In a time of stupidity, the smart person is king. This may not be the reality yet, but that does not mean we cannot make it reality. This book, this bible, is designed to encourage ignorant people and those who are already-informed to think and rethink. It is designed to make everyone see the world from a different point of view. It is designed to give a voice to those who want to say something, but cannot. It is designed to make you laugh, make you mad, make you scream and make you change the world.

Welcome to the Church of Fuck You.

The Church of Fuck You
Bible
Holy Shit Edition

The Church of Fuck You Bible: *Holy Shit Edition*

If you purchase this book without a cover you should be aware that this book may be stolen property and reported as "unsold and destroyed" to the publisher. In such cases neither the author nor the publisher has received any payment for this "stripped book".

Copyright © 2013 by Patrick Ellis

All rights reserved. No part of this book may be reproduced in any form or by any electronic or mechanical means, including information storage and retrieval systems, without permission in writing from the publisher, except by a reviewer who may quote brief passages in a review.

ISBN: 978-0-578-12545-9

Printed in the United States of America

Acknowledgements

I would like to thank everyone who has supported me and motivated me to start this Church and to write this bible.

I would specifically like to thank all the people who have followed me, whether they followed my daily posts and/or my videos. Thank you for all your support and thank you for your encouragement when I needed it.

I would like to thank all my critics. Please keep putting me down. It makes me work harder to prove you wrong.

I would like to thank all the stupid people in the world. Without your ridiculous behavior, the Church may have never been created.

Lastly, I want to thank you for buying this book. I truly hope you enjoy it.

Chapters:

Genesis

Exodus

Job

Songs of St. Patrick

Proverbs

Psalms

Acts

Stupid People

Man Section (Asshole Time)

Contradictions in the Christian Bible

Counter Arguments

Fuck you's

What If

Revelation

Genesis

This chapter is not about the beginning of the world. This chapter will not include stories about sacrificing your children to a god, a floating zoo, incest, cities being destroyed for partying, humans and animals drowning in floods, including FISH, or any of the usual suspects in genesis chapters. That would just be fucking ridiculous for a book to include such ludicrous stories.

No, this chapter is something completely different, although maybe equally ridiculous. This is about the beginning of me, the beginning of my mind, and the creation of the church.

For as long as I can remember, I have had a unique perspective, a lens through which I viewed the world. Let me give you an example of how my brain operates. Do you remember the L.A. riots? This was right after the Rodney King case and the police were found not guilty. Now, how they were found not guilty is beyond me, since they had been caught on fucking tape beating the shit out of the guy…but that is a story for another day. So, cops were acquitted and everyone goes nuts. They take to the streets and begin to destroy everything. Some people were praising the riots. Some people said they understood the rioters' frustrations. I personally thought it was the dumbest thing in the world.

Of course, I understood the anger and the frustration of the people. What I did not understand, however, was the reaction. Who gets mad at something they feel is unjust and begins to break their own shit? It would be the equivalent of your employer doing something really bad to you and in retaliation you go into the parking lot and beat the shit out of your own car. How is that hurting your employer? Same premise as the L.A. riots. They got mad at "the man", but subsequently go into their own neighborhood, burning down their own houses, breaking in their own stores, and destroying their own streets. For the life of me I did not understand how this was to accomplish anything. And it was indeed fruitless, of course.

That is how my brain works. I try to look at things from a logical standpoint. I look at situations from different angles and determine if what is being done is smart, fair, equal, or justified. I look for contradictions or inequalities. In short, I try to look past the surface and dig deeper into the situation, regardless of the situation.

I love to challenge conventional wisdom and everyone's "Moral Code" as well. I find myself struggling to believe people when they say, "I would never do this" or "I would never do that." I have found that throughout my life people will do damn near anything given the right situation (or wrong situation, depending on how you want to look at it). People will punch their mother in the throat if something happened that warranted it. I know some of you may be thinking that nothing could ever happen that would cause you to punch your mother in the throat. Oh really? Well, what if your mother was trying to kill you because she was told by god that the world was ending and she was trying to spare you from the wrath of her god? Could you punch her in the throat then? What if she was trying to kill your children? Could you strike her then? What if she unplugged your game before you had a chance to save it or ate the last ice cream sandwich and left the box in the freezer? You might go in the freezer to get an ice cream sandwich, but all you find is an empty box. Can you kung-fu her ass then?

One of the reasons I challenge moral codes is because there is no universal moral code. It is all an illusion. I believe that you should not kill someone; but, if you break into my house, threaten my life or the life of my immediate family, that code is out the fucking window. I feel you should not steal; but, if a family is starving, I would understand, even support, someone stealing food to feed their children.

I think that is what I want the world to understand. It is not just black and white on a lot of issues. Many issues have a gray area that most people pretend does not exist. Now I will admit that with certain issues- killing, molesting, raping children, for example - there is no gray area. Outside a small list of only a few things, the world lives in a twisted gray area that anyone would venture into given the right or wrong situation.

So, now that you have a little insight as to how I think, you can start to see how this church came about. Obviously, I abhor stupidity – it may be every-day nonsense or it may be illogical societal trends. This is why the Church was started. It began as a way to vent frustration, but it has become much bigger than that.

The Church is the place where you can be who you are. I do not care what religion you claim or if you claim one at all, what your sexual preference is, what color or ethnicity you happen to be - you are welcome here. The Church is a place that requires you to think for yourself and to think outside of the box. The Church is a place where you can express your views and your views will always be welcomed as long as they are intelligent and well-thought out. The Church is a place where you can laugh and laugh at the world. Most importantly, the Church is a place where you can be free from all the bullshit. That is the Church that I have created and that is the Church that I want people to feel proud of.

Exodus

The Ten Commandments

For those of you who are familiar with the Christian bible, you know that the Ten Commandments are in Exodus. I do not see the point in rewriting that long, rather boring chapter. I would prefer to talk specifically about the Ten Commandments. My Ten Commandments. These are not rules, but more like guidelines on how to live your life. You can create your own rules or guidelines if you would like. I have mine and here they are:

1. **You must strive to make this world a better place.** I do not believe a god exists to solve our problems. I do not believe a government entity can fix the world. It is up to us, all of us. If prayer could fix the world, it would have been fixed by now. There are governments galore in the world and things only seem to get worse. It is up to us, a vast collection of individuals, who should strive to make the world better for ourselves, our children and the generations yet to come. Whether you help to make the entire world better or stick to local and community ventures, your job is to make the world better. You owe it to those that came before you and to those that will come after you to make this chaotic mess a better place than when you entered it.

2. **You must be yourself and only yourself.** You should never change to fit another's image of what they feel you should be. You should never hide yourself because you feel like someone will not like

or accept who you are. You should never change yourself to fit in with the crowd. You should be you and only you. If someone cannot accept who you are, fuck them.

3. **Bigotry is never acceptable.** I do not mind you hating something or someone. Hating someone because they have done wrong to you or because they are an asshole is fine and perfectly acceptable. Hating someone because of their skin color, sexual preference, religious choices or any other idiotic standard is fucking retarded. You should never be a bigot and when possible, openly speak out against bigotry.

4. **Think for yourself.** Regardless of what you want to believe, know why you believe it. There are too many people in the world that believe shit because they were told to believe it or scared into believing it. You should not be one of those people. Whether you believe in a god, evolution, creationism or the motherfucking spaghetti monster, believe because of your own conviction- it belongs to you, no one else. Do not believe something because you are supposed to or because it is fashionable. This extends to beliefs outside of religious- non-religious beliefs as well. Convictions in politics, social issues, any issue- all of your beliefs should be an expression of yourself.

5. **Treat others as you expect to be treated.** We have all heard the saying, "Do unto others..." Well, it is a pretty damn good saying. If you want respect, you have to give respect. If you want honesty, you must be honest. If you want faithfulness, you must be faithful. It is amazing to me how many people feel they can mistreat someone and that someone will not respond in a negative way. Do not be misled. Know that however you treat someone else; you should expect the exact same treatment in return.

6. **Have a backbone.** While there are some that will return the treatment they receive back to the person that is giving it, there are plenty of those that will not. They allow people to treat them in any fashion and they never say a word. Whether it is a loved one, a boss, a coworker or even a complete stranger, they allow any and every one to run over top of them. Again, you cannot be this type of person. You must stand up for yourself and demand respect. I am not telling you to curse out your boss or get into fist fights when anyone approaches you wrong. What I am telling you is that you should demand that people always treat you with respect. That is never negotiable.

7. **Have a foundation of logic and common sense.** We are human. We are going to do illogically shit at times. We are going to love people inexplicably.

There are going to be times where our thoughts make no earthly sense. We are going to have fears that are flat out stupid. It is a part of being human. What we should not do is base our entire existence on illogical shit. We should use reasoning to survive and become better people. We must use our brains to create a better society, a better world.

8. **Learn to laugh.** Not only should you learn to laugh at the world around you, you should learn to laugh at yourself. We all know the saying, "Laughter is the best medicine". Albeit, if your leg is chopped off, it will not matter how much you laugh, it is not going to bring your leg back. What laughter can indeed do is improve your mind and body. There is a great deal of health benefits to laughing. It reduces stress. It improves vascular blood flow. It lowers blood pressure. It increases memory and learning ability. It helps your body fight off disease and infections. I could go on and on, but you get the point.

9. **Work for what you want.** There is nothing worse in this world than a lazy ass person who wants everything easy and free. If you want something in life, you should work to get it. Do not live your life looking for handouts and leeching off hard working people. You should want more out of life than being a charity case.

10. Karma is a bitch. I know there are plenty of those who do not believe in anything. They believe life just happens. Typically, I would agree with them. On this issue though, I have to disagree. I do not believe in a god or any divine being manipulating the world to his or her desire. I do, however, believe in what goes around, comes around. I have witnessed this happen far too many times. To tell you a quick story, there was a time in my life where I lost my job. My less-than-wonderful wife at the time gave me shit constantly for being down on my luck. Apparently, without a job I was less than nothing. A mutual acquaintance at that time agreed with her wholeheartedly. He piled on as much as possible. I was not a man, I was worthless, and I was a nobody. Well, about six months later that same mutual someone lost their job. A certain someone's lady at the time started giving him very familiar shit because he was without employment. Now, he was less than nothing. He was not a man and his wife made sure to remind him on a regular basis. This drove him insane. It seems when you are down, having someone kick you does not help the situation. Who knew? You want to hear the kicker? Guess who this motherfucker had the nerve to call for comfort? Me indeed! Again, karma is a bitch. It has a way of throwing all the things you do and say right back in your face. Respect Karma.

As I stated above, these are my Ten Commandments. Living by these rules or guidelines does not ensure that you are going to have a perfect life. It does, however, ensure that you are taking the proper steps to, in my opinion, be happy, worthwhile, and to live a respectable life.

Job

If you are looking for a story about a man getting tormented by a bored-ass god and devil, then you are in the wrong place. This is not that story. If you are curious about how sick and twisted a god could potentially be, you should read that aforementioned story, though. Supposedly, this god allowed a man to lose everything- wealth, health and children- just to prove a point. He did nothing wrong. He was busy living when god and Satan decided to manipulate his existence. Sick and twisted is right! Immoral (isn't that ironic? God is immoral?).

This chapter is not the bible chapter Job. It is job. J.O.B. As in, something you work and get money for. In this chapter, we are going to talk about a number of different things concerning your job.

The first thing I want to talk about is how to act at the job. We will call this work etiquette. Ready? Here we go:

Go to work! – People who always call out sick or find excuses not to go to work drive me crazy. If you have a job, please take your ass to work. There are a lot of people that would love to have your job. Do not take it for granted and abuse your company simply because they will not fire you out of fear of getting sued. No one cares if you screw over the company because no one cares about rich people. What people do care about, especially your co-workers, is having to do two jobs (your job and their job) while only getting paid for one.

Fucking work, at work! – When you come to work, please do your fucking job. Work is not supposed to be the time to handle all of your personal business. No one cares if you take a personal call, send a personal e-mail, pay a bill or look shit up on-line. Well, no one cares as long as it does not affect them. If you are talking on the phone all day about your bad-ass children or your cheating-ass husband, and want to start handing out your work at 4:30 because you leave at 5:00 and you do not have the time to do it, we have a serious problem. If you are talking on the phone all day and now no one can take a personal call because of new rules aimed at your behavior, we have a serious problem. If you are e-mailing all day and now the company is checking all e-mails in response to your behavior, we have a serious problem. If the company blocked internet access because you were constantly caught tending to your virtual farm or doing a virtual drive-by with your virtual gangster, I will non-virtually choke the shit out of you.

Leave your drama at home! - We all have problems. We have all dealt with health issues, death in the family, relationship problems, stress from children, money issues- the list goes on and on. Leave that shit at home though. Even if you work with your husband or wife, parent or child, leave that shit at home. You are coming to work to do a job. All that outside drama needs to be left outside. Typically, your co-workers have nothing to do with your bad night or bad life. Do not take your bullshit out on them or the rest of the office.

Leave your drama at home! Part 2 – Again, we all have problems, and yet, in addition to those problems, at almost every job we have to deal with a drama queen. This is the person that has to tell the entire company every bad thing that goes on in their life. According to them, the world is ending every day. Everyone can expect a life changing story from this person, especially on Mondays. They apparently have the worst life in the history of lives on Mondays. If are you a drama queen, please do the rest of the office a favor and shut the fuck up. We do not want to hear depressing-ass stories every day. We just want to do our job and go home. Do us a favor and allow us to do our job in peace.

Kicking up dust – We seem to all have people at our place of employment that like to keep drama going. They are the ones that take a small conversation or a small situation and turn it into Armageddon. They love to tell people what someone said or did in hopes that the person will get angry and start a confrontation. These are the people that love to spread gossip. They are the ones that love to start chaos. Do yourself a favor and stay away from these people. Even if you did not say anything, your name will come up. It is best to keep your distance and hope for no honorable mentions. If you happen to be this lunatic, get a life.

Shower! – There is no rhyme or reason why you should ever come to work funky. Even if you have a late night, you should still wash your ass and brush your teeth. There is nothing worse than sitting next to someone at work who is foul. Come on man.

Tattle tale! Really?! – It is amazing to me that every job has an employee that runs and tells the boss everything about anyone in a 3 mile radius. They make it seem like it is their personal duty to report everything that goes on in the department. If you know this person at your company, avoid them at all costs. Believe me when I tell you, they are going to catch you on the wrong day and you are going to get in trouble for threatening them or assaulting them. To prevent that, avoid them. If you happen to be the tattle tale, go fuck yourself.

Mind your business – At every job there seems to be one human being that feels the need to live vicariously through other people at the job. People, mind your own fucking business. Stop eavesdropping on conversations or trying to read people's private e-mails –do not worry about anyone else unless they are willfully sharing information with you. Bottom line, you need to get a life of your own.

Show Mercy – One of the things I find funny at a job is when you fuck up, you want everyone to remember that you are human and you make mistakes. When someone else fucks up, they need to "do their god damn job or be retrained or fired". When you mess up, you want forgiveness. When a coworker messes up, you want their head. How about we remember that everyone is human and everyone will fuck up sometimes? Be compassionate- everyone has been in the imperfect position.

There are a number of different things that I do not understand that seem to happen in every work place. Among the worst things that I have ever seen, but see on a regular basis, are companies hiring supervisors off the street, having the supervisors' staff train them, and then place them into a supervisory role. How in the world can you supervise a person who trained you on how to do your job?

I also do not understand why employers put employees on the phone that cannot speak English. On what planet is that a good idea? Do you realize how frustrating it is to have to repeat the same shit over and over again? Do you realize how frustrating it is to have to say "What" twenty times because you cannot understand what the hell the other person is saying on the phone? I am not blaming the workers. They are just trying to do their job. I blame the manager or supervisor who decided that it was a good idea. If you hate talking to your employee because you cannot understand them, how in the hell do you think your customers feel?

I hate horrible managers. I loathe managers that do not work. You all know the managers that sit back and watch employees kill themselves while they sip coffee and talk to other managers about their weekend or their shoes. I cannot take seriously managers that have no idea what you do or cannot perform the job that you do. How in the world can you be a manager of an office and you cannot do any of the jobs within the office? You hardly ever see that shit in retail. You walk into a fast food place and the manager is running the register, cooking the fries, bagging up food and sweeping the floor, all at the same time. You walk into some offices and the managers can barely work their fucking computer.

I despise the managers who are on a daily power kick. These are the managers that have to bring up the fact that they are 'the manager' every 15 seconds. They throw their title around because it makes them feel important and special. These managers act like they are in the military and try to pull rank, showing a constant need to flex their muscles. They talk to people as if they are below them because, in their words, "You work for me." These are the managers that generally get their ass whooped by an employee who they caught on the wrong day.

I will leave you with this. I understand that everyone has to work. Well, those of us who want to actually contribute to society and not leech off the system, have to work. Do not let your job stress you. No job is worth your dignity or your sanity. I will never tell you to quit your job, but I will tell you is life is too short to be miserable. If your job is making you miserable, it is time for a change.

Sorry, last thing. For all the assholes that make work intolerable: Fuck You.

Songs of St. Patrick

Ex Wife

I remember the day; very clearly, I confessed my love to you
We walked down the aisle, I saw your smile and we said 'I do'
I loved you more than I loved myself, you were my entire life
And nothing made me happier than for you to be my wife

Our life was good, it started great, and I never saw the switch
I woke up one day and suddenly you became a bitch
My dream, my plans, my everything, always included us
Now I hope you cross the street and meet a metro bus

I can't believe how bad we got, it truly is a shame
I don't care what you say, you can give me all the blame
I'm tired of you, I'm tired of us, there's no need to talk
See you in court, sign the papers, outline this marriage in chalk.

Never

Never say I love you, unless you really mean it.
Never say you saw something, unless you've really seen it.
Never repeat what you heard, unless you know it's true
Never say you miss someone, unless you really do.

Never say that you are sick, unless you're really ill
Never vow to protect someone, unless you'll really kill
Never ask a question, unless you expect the truth
Never believe what someone says, unless you see the proof

Never brag about your plans, unless you will follow through
Never show respect to someone, unless they show respect you
Never call the police for help, unless you are really scared
Never cry over a person's death, unless you really cared

Never say you're sorry, unless you were in the wrong
Never sing the words out loud, unless you know the song
Never fold pocket jacks, unless someone goes all in
Never be the first to swing, unless you know you'll win

Never trust a picture, unless you've met face to face
Never trash a destination, unless you've visited that place
Never plan to be alone, unless you want to be
Never think you are perfect, unless you're a saint like me.

Religion

Only in religion, is asking a question wrong
Where you listen to some boring shit that last three hours long
Where treating a woman like a slave is considered love
Where pointless people feel empowered from something up above

Only in religion, your logic you concede
Where belief, without proof is all you'll ever need
Where doing nothing, is doing something, because you say you prayed
Where talking shit, in a nice suit, can definitely get you paid.

Only in religion, is common sense a lie
Where people live their entire life just waiting around to die
Where everyone is considered evil, except the people you say
Where murderers are always welcomed, as long as they aren't gay

Only in religion, do they serve death in a cup
And a book can manipulate people into blowing each other up
Where killing innocent people will get you constant praise
And you run around constantly screaming, these the last days

Only in religion, is brainwashing a child cool
They can be a fool as long as god is in their school
They can't do simple math, hell, they can hardly read
And the parents don't seem to care cause "God is all they need!"

Only in religion, do invisible beings need money
And respecting all beliefs is a concept that is funny
Where science is only useful to prove that god is real
And the ability to think on your own is the first thing that they kill

Only in religion, can the blind be healed with spit
And most every member is a fucking hypocrite
Where being a bigot is perfectly fine, because your way is true
And you can judge the entire world, but they can't judge you

Now I can go on for days and days, talking about these sheep
And exposing them for who they are is a promise I intend to keep
Whether you choose to believe it or not, well, that's your decision
But from me, and my entire church, fuck all religions.

True Love

My love for you, can't be measured, there's no need to try
My love for you, can't be healthy, surely I will die
But I don't care; you are mine, and mine you will stay
I'll hold you dear, in my heart, until my dying day.

Your color's perfect, shape divine, you're soft to the touch
If it's a crime, then lock me up, for loving you too much
But it's your looks, it's your warmth, your taste that is to blame
And any man that's ever met you surely feels the same

They can't have you, that's for sure, I won't let you go
I'm too possessive, too in love, I'll let the world know
That I'd kill a motherfucker for trying to take what's taken
Hands up, close your mouth, step away from my god damn bacon!

Proverbs

1

1. The world is not mature enough to live with a religion, but they are not mature enough to live without one.
2. Do not celebrate an asshole when they die. If they were an asshole when they were alive, being dead does not change that.
3. $200 shoes; $300 purse; $50 watch; $175 necklace; $250 in rings; $325 hairdo; $10 in your bank account = A Fucking Idiot.
4. Your car should not look better than your house, you should never look better than your children and your body should never be better than your mind.
5. Never let a broke person tell you how to get rich. If it was that easy, their broke ass would be doing it.
6. If people cannot accept you for who you are, then fuck them. If someone wants you to be someone else, tell them to go find someone else.
7. Gambling is only fun when you are winning. When you lose your money, it fucking sucks.
8. Life is not a sprint, it is a marathon. Run it too quickly and be rendered useless.
9. Life is too short to waste on pointless people. Cut them out of your life, so that you can have a life.
10. All a leech will do is drain a host dry. If you want more in life, get rid of the leeches in your life.
11. A friend pushes you forward, not hold you back. If your "friends" are not helping you get ahead in life, they are not your friends.

12. A woman who demands that a man spends money on her before she has sex with him is still a prostitute. She just gets payment in a different form.
13. A man who would cheat on his beautiful wife with an ugly chick = What is the fucking point?
14. Unless your problem is that you need $10, getting on your knees is not a solution. If you want change or a resolution, stand on your feet and make it happen.
15. Loose is something that is not firm or tightly fixed in place. Lose is to not win, to be defeated. Calling someone a looser is idiotic of epic propositions because while you are trying to insult someone, you are showing them just how fucking stupid you are

2

1. Give a guy a prostitute and he is happy for a day. Give a guy a wife and in 5 years half of his shit will be gone.
2. If a man shows you love by putting his fist into your face, show him you love him back by taking a hammer to his nuts.
3. Two double cheeseburgers, large fries, two apple pies, large chocolate shake and a diet coke = What is the fucking point?
4. The gun did not invent the desire to kill. The desire to kill invented the gun.
5. People who do not know the difference between your and you're or their/there/they're, yet complain when foreigners do not know English = A Fucking Idiot

6. Living your life with only the anticipation of an afterlife renders your life meaningless.
7. Terrorism is terrorism. The definition does not change because the person committing the act has on a suit and not a turban.
8. Being cute does not entitle you to be a bitch. Pretty girls can receive a hearty 'Fuck You' just like ugly girls can.
9. Sports are for entertainment purposes. If you get clinically depressed over a game that you did not play in or bet on, you need to get a life.
10. Using big words only make you seem smart if you use them correctly.
11. Saying "I'm sorry" does nothing to ease the pain felt from the death of a loved one. If you do not know what to say, it is best to say nothing.
12. If you want something broken, give it to a two year old.
13. If a woman would suck a stranger's dick in a bathroom of a club, but would not step in a puddle in the same bathroom because that is nasty, she = A Fucking Idiot.
14. Asshole (I just put this in here so that you can say "Proverbs 2:14" and call someone an asshole, without actually calling someone an asshole. Great for work.)
15. There are a vast number of people that believe in a heaven and a hell. There were a vast number of people who believed the earth was flat. There were a vast number of people who believed slavery was right. Just because a lot of people believe it, does not mean it is true.

3

1. Never invite a thief into your house and leave them by themselves. If they steal something, it is your fault, not theirs.
2. Women, never introduce your man to a girl you know is a whore. If she tries to sleep with him, it is your fault, not hers.
3. Just because you believe a person who is known to lie, does not mean they are a good liar. It just means you are too stupid to recognize bullshit.
4. Know who people are and treat them accordingly. Just because someone is your friend, that does not mean they magically become a different person around you.
5. If a lesbian is supposed to be attracted only to women, why do lesbians date women who look and act like men?
6. If a gay man is looking to attract another gay man, why would they dress up and act like a woman?
7. If you are old enough to shoot a gun, throw a grenade, drive a tank or shoot a missile, than you should be old enough to buy a six pack and drink it.
8. Have you noticed that the good people in this world seem to die young while the assholes seem to live forever?
9. If your children get you food stamps, public housing, daycare vouchers and a cell phone, are you really taking care of your children? Or are your children taking care of you?

10. Going to a church in search of knowledge is the equivalent of going to a KKK meeting in search of racial harmony.
11. Any government that requires you get a license to fish, or to hunt, or to drive, or to sell merchandise, but does not require you to obtain a license to have a child, has some fucked up priorities.
12. Is there one good reason why we spend more money on war and the military than we do on education?
13. Son of a Bitch! (Again, an inside joke for church members. When your boss puts extra work on your desk or you come home and the house is a mess. Just say Proverbs 3:13)
14. Sex is great for your health. It is a great way to burn calories and lose weight. So, do not hesitate to tell someone to go fuck themselves.
15. Do not live to work, work to live.

4

1. When your life is engulfed in flames, those that love you will do their best to get you out of the fire. Those that do not will simply stand by and watch you burn.
2. When you break up with someone, why do they say, "You will never find another one like me"? If I did not want your ass, why would I want to find another one like you?
3. Saying "I'm sorry" after doing something once generally implies that you will not do it again. Saying

"I'm sorry" after doing something for the fifth time means you are not saying sorry for what you did. You are just sorry that you got caught, again.
4. You can always discover a lie by paying attention to the details of the story. If the details seem to change, there is something wrong.
5. What is the difference between 10 people killed at one time, at one location and 10,000 people killed throughout the year? One is labeled a national tragedy and the other is just a statistic.
6. If you only care about facts when the facts prove your point, you are truly brainwashed.
7. If you have already chosen a side before a discussion, then what is the point of the discussion?
8. If you are too old to play like a child, then perhaps you are too old to have children.
9. Remember your target audience. If you trying to reach people who cannot read, making a sign telling them to call you is a bad idea.
10. Never piss off the person who is cooking or handling your food.
11. Some religions believe that their god is a healer. If that is the case, why do they go to the hospital? Either they lack faith or they realize there is only so much you can accomplish when living outside of reality.
12. Screaming during an argument does not magically make you right. If you are wrong, the only thing yelling does is allow more people to know that you are an idiot.

13. $2,000 stereo system; $5,000 rims; $200 tinted windows; $3,000 in body work; needing to borrow money to put gas in your car = A Fucking Idiot.
14. Fuck you (my favorite Proverb. You know I am going to say this, a lot!)
15. Cheaters will not always cheat. Liars will not always lie. The problem is when you do it once it is hard to believe that you will not do it again.

5

1. While having sex, if your girl's body is not tight, shaking or trembling, you are doing something wrong.
2. I would rather bus tables for a living and be happy than to work a high paying job and live in misery.
3. Laws that are passed, but not enforced, are about as good as taking a blind man sightseeing.
4. If you are only with a man for his money or a woman for her looks, then you deserve all the bullshit that comes your way.
5. It is amazing how someone who has never left the state they live in, can think they know what the world is like.
6. It is interesting how everything the media says is true, unless they are talking bad about your political party, then they are full of shit and should never be trusted.
7. In the world where information is readily available, being ignorant of something is a personal choice.

8. Beware of the man that is selling you something that they do not want.
9. People who live beyond their means will always be broke.
10. There is a saying that "You cannot have your cake and eat it too." Well, what the fuck is the point of having a cake if you cannot eat it?
11. Working at a job you hate to pay for things you cannot afford is not living. Staying in a house you do not like with a person you like even less is not living. Hanging with friends who treat you bad while dealing with a family that treats you worse is not living. If you are not living, it is time to make changes in your life.
12. Allow your children to be children during their childhood. It is the only one they have.
13. Waiting until a person dies to say how you really feel is stupid. If you do not say it while they are alive, then do not say it at all.
14. Just because you agree with what someone says, does not mean they are intelligent. The simple truth could be that you both are idiots.
15. The first day you decide to stop feeding your mind, is the day you have truly died.

Psalms

Psalms, in this book, is a section to lift your spirits. This is an attempt to provide the motivation you may need if you find yourself down or to push you ahead when you feel you cannot go on. Read them once, or read them every day if you need to. This section is for all the people who need that shot in the arm to get them going or keep them going.

Your dreams:

Everyone has dreams, but few people truly go after them. Many quit and settle for whatever life has to offer them. You will not be one of those people. You will go after your dreams and you will accomplish anything you put your mind to. You have not failed until you quit trying. Do not quit trying. You will make it. You will be everything you ever wanted to be, and then some. You will make it to the top and you will look back on all the people that had said you will fail, and laugh your ass off.

You will pass people on your road to success who have quit on their dreams. They will look at you in disgust, angered at you because you dare to dream and dream big. They will be upset because you have not given up dreaming. You have not forfeited your future and have not accepted that your role in the world is less than extraordinary - it confuses those people. They do not understand why you are chasing your dream and they do not. Needless to say, fuck those people. They will never understand you because they do not have your drive, your heart, your courage to follow a dream. They do not have your ambition. All they have is remorse. Let them dwell in their bitterness. You have more important things to do than worry about people that do not matter. Remember, only you can stop you. And you are not dumb enough to do that.

Your love:

There are people in this world that love misery. They love when people fail, especially marriages or "true love". They love the drama of a failing relationship. They love the hopelessness couples feel when their relationship is spiraling out of control. You will not fall prey to their joy. You will make any loving relationship work despite the assholes cheering for it to fail. You know your love. Your love knows you. You two can make it work, no matter what. As long as you two stand by each other and give it your all, there is no problem that you two cannot overcome.

Your job:

First of all, let us get this out of the way. Fuck your boss. Fuck any person at your job that tries to make your life miserable at work. If you do not like your job, do not worry about it. You are only there to pay the bills while you work on your dream. It happens to be something to exercise the brain until your plans take off. You will not be there forever and those bitter ass people know it. They see your potential and they hate it. They know they will be stuck at the bullshit job for the rest of their lives, while you will be off living your dream and doing whatever it is that makes you happy. So, if you have a bad day at work, do not fret. Just use it to keep you motivated to make your dreams come true.

Down on your luck:

There are times in every person's life when they hit a wall. It may seem like this will last forever. Trust me, it will not. If you hit hard times, keep pushing on. You push and you push until you knock that wall down. Nothing will stand in your way. Nothing can hold you down. You cannot lie down and die like a wounded dog. You will continue to strive and you will get out of this. You will be stronger when you make it out. You will be smarter. More importantly, you will never need to read this again because you will know, without a shadow of a doubt, that you could do everything again if you needed to.

To leave:

I know leaving can be scary. You may be afraid to be alone. You may be scared that half of your check will be taken. You may not know how to live by yourself. Believe me when I tell you, you will make all necessary changes. You can make it on your own. You can survive and you will survive. You owe it to yourself to be happy. Life is far too short to spend even an hour with someone that does not deserve your time, your energy, your love.

And for women in an abusive relationship, you have to pack up and go. This is not even a question. You deserve to have someone in your life that loves you and treats you with respect. You deserve to be happy and safe in your home. You should not have to live in fear - no one should. And if you have children, you owe it to them to leave. No child should have to witness physical harm between parents. Do not let fear keep you in dangerous situation. Fuck him and fuck the unknown. I know that you can make it without that jackass. You just have to realize it. The day you realize that you do not deserve to be a punching bag will be the day you truly begin to live the rest of your life.

For men living with a bitch of a spouse, you owe it to yourself to leave. Do not worry about the money. Fuck the money. You would be an idiot to stay with a person that makes you miserable because of anything material. Pay that bitch and move on with life. There is another person in this world that will appreciate you, that will love you for who you are, but you will not find that person because you are wasting precious time being married to a selfish asshole. Dump that broad and go find someone that will treat you right. You can do it. I know you can. You just have to believe it.

Losing a loved one:

I know this time is hard. I know there are not too many things that you want to hear or read right now. There is nothing that anyone can say that will ease the pain. There is nothing that anyone can do to truly comfort you. So, I will not give you words of comfort, I will give you words of strength. You will make it through this. You will cry your tears. You will ask why. You will grieve. Soon though, the pain will ease and you will start to put the pieces of your life together again. You will never forget the person you lost, and you should not. You will always remember them and if you want to honor them, you honor them by living your life and making every day count. You will honor them by going on. You will honor them by smiling again, one day. You will honor them by laughing again, one day. That person you lost would surely not want to cause you pain. The one you lost would not want you to live in misery. And you will not, because you loved them too much to do that to them.

The light from their life, through your memories, will make your life brighter even in their absence.

Acts

How to Act in a Restaurant

There are many different rules on how to act in a restaurant. It does not matter what type of restaurant you are in, these rules would apply to them all. This is sort of a universal rulebook on Restaurant Etiquette. So, when you go to a restaurant, please observe the following rules:

1. Please keep your conversation at your table. The entire restaurant does not need to hear everything you say.

2. Do not be an asshole to the staff, especially the waiter. Not only is it good manners to be polite, but you never fuck with people that handle your food. NEVER!

3. Control your children. If they are not old enough for a restaurant, then find a babysitter or stay your ass at home.

4. Get off your fucking cell phone. It is just flat out rude to the people you are eating dinner with and/or the people around you.

5. Tip! Waiters make the majority of their money from tips. Do not be a cheap ass. Even if the wait service was lacking, still kick them a few bucks.

6. If you must complain, do it in a nice way. If they fuck up, which can happen, make the error known, but do not be a dick about it.

7. Do not be a slob. A little trash at your table is understandable and expected. They should not have to close down the table after you leave to clean up and repaint your section.

8. No sex shit at the table. If you want to get a couple of kisses and hugs and cuddle at your table, that is perfectly acceptable. If you are moaning and panting and all that extra shit, then we have a problem. I came to the restaurant to eat my chicken, not to smell your fish.

9. Pay your bill. If you cannot afford to eat at a restaurant, then do not take your broke ass to that restaurant. Skipping out on a bill hurts the restaurant, but it royally fucks your waitress/waiter. A lot of restaurants make them pay for your bill and if it is a slow night, they can actually work eight hours and lose money. That shit is not cool.

10. No arguing or fighting. People generally go to restaurants to relax, eat and have a good time. They do not go there to see adults fussing and yelling at each other like twelve year olds. If you are not mature enough to go out without getting into some kind of verbal or physical altercation, then stay the fuck home.

How to Act On the Internet

The internet can be a wonderful thing. It can be a place where you can conduct research, connect with long lost friends or family members, meet new friends, pay bills, book plane tickets – it can be a remarkably useful and far-reaching tool. It can also be a nightmare. There are a number of things that happen on the internet every day that are just maddening. As a result of this reality, we have to include internet etiquette in this holiest of holy bibles.

First of all, the internet seems to make people unbelievably tough or rich or sexy… or whatever other fantasy people want to create about themselves. Mainly, this occurs because they do not think people will be able to call them out on their bullshit. Be who you are, people. Do not blow yourself up on the internet because you know no one will be able to tell the difference.

It is amazing how many people on-line make $100,000 a year, have a supermodel wife or a Greek god-like body. The more you are on-line, the more you realize how full of shit this world really is. That, or how sad and depressed a lot of people must be to have to go online and write a fictional story of their life – from accomplishments to character - to make themselves feel important.

Another phenomena the internet produces are the internet gangsters and racist pricks showing up online. Regardless of the story, you will always find a "stupid nigger" reply in the comment section. You will always find someone spouting ignorant shit online. You will always find someone saying how they will "fuck you up cuz I'z 100% real deal u don't wanna c me bitch azz nicca!" (I feel my IQ dropping from having to write that stupid shit)

Bottom line, stupidity is rampant on the internet. Quick rules on how to act on the internet:

1. Be yourself. Do not create an alter ego simply because you are behind a keyboard.

2. Please, be able to type a complete sentence and spell correctly. Your point, regardless of how valid that point is, is not effective if people have to use a military-style decoder to interpret what you say.

3. Forwarding an e-mail or sharing a picture or link changes nothing. If you want change, you actually have to do something.

4. Fuck the racists and internet gangsters. They are not worth your time or energy.

How to Act like a Man

This is such an open-ended statement. Acting like a man seems to change depending on whom you talk to and want they want you to do. I was with a woman once that defined a man as someone who would stay with a woman regardless of how shitty she treated him. Needless to say, that bitch was crazy. There are some people that feel a real man loves Jesus.

This in itself is hilarious because one of the largest and most homophobic organizations in the world feels that in order to be a real man you must be in love with another man. Some people feel that a real man never hits a woman, regardless of the situation. Those people are idiots. Some people feel that a real man controls his woman. He keeps her under his finger and controls everything that she does in her life. I should not even have to say how stupid this is, but I will. This is stupid.

So, what do I feel a man should act like? Well, first and foremost, a man should be himself. In order to do that a man first must know who he is and never try to be someone he is not. Men do not have time to play pretend. You will never see a man standing on a corner, playing gangster. Now, I am not knocking those who hit the streets to earn their living. What I am knocking are the grown ass men who hang on a street corner all day without there being money involved. I am knocking the men who are over 30, living in their parents' house and having no plans to leave. Basically, real men are not useless. Real men are not lazy. Real men contribute to society.

Real men are honest. They have no reason to lie. Real men do not have to advertise who they are. If you are a man, you should never have to go around talking about how you keep it "100%". There is no other alternative, so this mindless repetition is unnecessary. Real men do not put up with bullshit. They do not have the time or patience for it. Real men would never let a woman run over top of him or control him. A real man would never abuse a woman. However, he should protect himself and his children from anything or anyone, including a crazy woman. He might go as far as to hit a woman if he feels his or his children's life is in danger.

Another thing I wanted to touch on is real men take care of their children. I do not care if "baby mama" is insane. I do not care if she tries to make life unbearable. I do not care if she takes you to court, lies her ass off, and tries to take all of your money. You have to be there for your children. It is not their fault you picked a psycho bitch to impregnate. It is not their fault that mom is trying to make your life miserable. You have to be there for them. You have to show them that you love them and nothing will ever change that. I know it is hard. Believe me when I tell you, I know it is hard, but you have to do it. You owe it to your children to be that man.

This is what I feel a real man is. It is not something that can be defined easily and it is not something that will be a universal definition of a "Real Man". As I said, the definition changes depending on whom you are talking to and what they expect from men. For me, I think a man should be happy, productive in life and takes care of his responsibilities. So, I tailor my definition to fit that thought.

How to Act like an Adult

There are some fundamental things that come along with being considered an adult. I will give you my opinion on what an adult should be and do. First and foremost, an adult is able to take care of themselves and their children, both physically and financially. If you have a mental or physical handicap or disability, then this does not apply to you. If you are able to work, but just choose to be lazy, then you are not an adult. If you are able to live on your own, but choose to live with your parents so that they can cook and clean for you, you are not an adult. If you are living off the system because you think the world is too hard for you to make it on your own, you are not an adult. I completely understand if you are facing hard times and need help. You may go back with your parents to get back on your feet. You may ask for government assistance to help you in your time of trouble. That is perfectly acceptable. What is not acceptable is for a grown ass person to not even attempt to make it on their own.

That is the most fundamental aspect of being an adult - responsibility. Adults are responsible for themselves and their actions. Adults do not make excuses as to why they could not do something. Adults do not blame the world, their parents, their past, "the man", or an ex for their failures. They realize that the ultimate responsibility for their life falls squarely on their shoulders.

Adults accept their mistakes and more importantly, learn from their mistakes. They do not repeat the same actions over and over, while expecting something to change. In case you did not know, that is the definition of insanity. They learn from their experiences and they continue to grow, as a person. They do not let their mistakes define them; they allow their mistakes to mold them into better people.

Another thing adults do is to continue to educate themselves and grow, mentally and intellectually. Only a fool feels they know everything. A lot of us have been that fool. We were teenagers and no one could tell us anything. We knew all about life and how everything works and we had a fool-proof plan to make it 'big'. Then we entered the real world and realized that we did not know shit. That is the first step to becoming an adult, realizing that you know nothing. The second step is to start learning all you need to know, and even things you do not think you need to know. Admitting you do not know something and taking the proper steps to learn it is a fundamental stage in adulthood.

Lastly, one thing that an adult will refuse to do is play childish games. I am not talking about board games or laser tag. I am talking about playing games with the lives of those around them. They do not have time to lie and cheat. They may not be faithful to one person, but adults establish that up front. They do not commit themselves to anyone if they are not ready. They do not make promises they do not intend to keep. They are real, upfront and have a "take me as I am" attitude. Yes, they will grow as people, but they will grow because they have decided that is what is best for them. They will not change simply for the sake of others' expectations - they will change due to a desire to become better people themselves.

How to act when drinking

There are a number of important things you need to keep in mind when you drink. One, and this is the most important, no drinking and driving. Too many people have died from some asshole driving drunk. It is simply not worth your life or the lives that you could take. You should call a cab or a friend or sleep it off. Do not get behind the wheel while intoxicated.

Number two; know what type of drunken person you are. If you want to fight when you drink, keep your ass at home and drink alone. If you get loud and act stupid, then do not drink in public places. If you get extremely horny, do not drink around ugly people or people you would not want to sleep with. If you get depressed and suicidal, do not drink at all.

Number three; know your limit. If you are drinking just to relax, then you may need a couple of beers or maybe a shot or two. Drinking a fifth of anything is not a good idea if you are not trying to get drunk.

Number four; drink what you can afford. Do not try to act like a big baller and order $500 bottles when you have $50 in your pocket. If you can afford vodka and orange juice, drink vodka and orange juice. If you can only afford soda, drink soda. If you can only afford water, keep your ass home.

There are other things that you should consider when you drink, especially if you are drinking around a group of people or at a club. Consideration for your friends or family is a must. It is not their job to babysit you all night. They should not have to worry about you laying in your own vomit or whether or not three dudes are about to run a train on you because you passed out on the couch. They should not have to stop you from trying to fight everyone in the club. They should not have to bail you out of jail because you were stalking some chick and she called the cops on you. If you are going out with friends to drink and have a good time, that is exactly what everyone is expecting to occur- a nice drink and a good time. Do not kill everyone's good time because you cannot handle your liquor and you refuse to cut yourself off.

Stupid People

There are a lot of stupid people walking among us and they, not surprisingly, do a lot of stupid shit. This chapter is dedicated to all of the stupid things that stupid people engage in. You may think that there are only a small number of stupid things that occur every day. You may think that, but you are way off target.

Crafting a world that condones stupidity:

We are living in a world where we cater to idiots. Have you checked some of the warning labels that companies are required to put on their products? The most offensive one to me is on the stroller for a baby. It warns the parent to remove the child from the stroller before closing it. What idiot would not do that? What numb skull would think it was a good idea to close the fucking stroller, and then take the child out? And more importantly, what society would think it is acceptable for this person to reproduce?

Not only do we allow these types of people to reproduce, we reward them for their stupidity. Why are companies required to put such labels on products? It is because if they do not and a parent closes their child in the stroller resulting in their child getting hurt, the parent can sue the company for not telling them the obvious – do not snap a stroller shut on your toddler!

We are living in a world where companies are not wise to assume that people have a fucking brain. This is the same reason for which companies have to put a warning label on an iron that says, "Do not iron the clothes while they are on your body". You have to actually tell people that it is a bad idea to put burning hot metal against their body. Companies cannot assume that a person will be smart enough to know that. They have to treat their consumers like idiots or get hit with a 50 million dollar lawsuit from some genius that ironed his pants while he was wearing them. He suffered severe burns to his legs and now someone must be held responsible. Of course we cannot hold the idiot responsible - that would be ludicrous! The company must be held responsible for not warning the idiot.

Some other favorites of mine are:

Do not use in the shower – Written on hair dryers

For external use only – Written on a curling iron

Caution: Hot beverages are hot! – Written on a coffee cup

Caution: Do not drive or operate heavy machinery – Written on children's cough syrup

Caution: Contents will be hot after cooking – Written on microwavable dinners

Warning: May cause drowsiness – Written on sleeping pills

I could go on for days and days with these warning labels, but you get the point. We must protect the idiots from themselves. Personally, I would rather remove all the warning labels and let the 'survival of the fittest' motto take over. We should not have to live in a world where we have to label a bag of peanuts with a warning label, "Product contains nuts". If you cannot figure that out, then you are on your own.

Relationship Nonsense:

There are so many ridiculous things that regularly happen in relationships, it is unreal. They say people do crazy things when they are in love. I would not use the word 'crazy' for every situation. Sometimes, it is just flat-out dumb. Other times, 'idiotic' would be a more appropriate word. For example, some of the questions that people ask in a relationship are unnecessarily obtuse. Have you ever been asked, "If you weren't with me, who would you be with?" In case you do not understand why this is a horrible question, let me explain. It is dumb because there is only one logical answer. That answer is, "no one." Any person you say will forever be engraved in your partner's mind. If that person was to come up in any way, in any form, the first thing that would enter your partner's mind would be, "That's the person you want to be with." Do not ask questions that are only designed to mind-fuck you. And for heaven's sake, do not answer those questions if they are ever asked. If you do not know what a set up question is, let me give you a few so that you can know what to look out for:

Do you think this makes me look fat? – Obvious answer, "No, not at all." Anything other than that and you can expect to have a conversation about her weight and why you do not find her attractive. Best answer to give, "No, the clothes do not make you look fat. The fat makes you look fat. The clothes just highlight it." Be prepared to duck.

Do you think she is prettier than me? – Again, bullshit question. The obvious answer is, "No, of course not." You can even go better and say something along the lines of, "No baby. No woman could ever be prettier than you." Best answer to give, "Have you looked in the mirror lately? Hell yeah she is prettier than you." Be prepared to get your own place.

Am I the best you have ever been with, sexually? – Gentlemen, do not ask this question. If she says yes, you will not believe her and if she says no, you will be crushed. Ladies, men will always tell you yes, even if you are not. It is a pointless question.

If I died, what….. – I personally hate this question. No matter what you say, it is the wrong answer. If you say you would grieve for years, the other person gets upset because they do not want you to be miserable. If you say you will grieve for a while, that is not enough grieving time. If you say you will not get remarried or find someone else, the other person gets upset because they do not want you to be alone. If you say you will remarry, all of a sudden you are plotting their death so you can find your next spouse. It is a no win situation. Best answer is, "I would party my ass off before you are even in the ground." Be prepared for an extended hospital stay.

Those are just a few examples and trust me when I tell you, there are plenty more. Please avoid these types of questions as all cost. They do nothing to add value to the relationship. They are just there to fuck relationships up.

Another dumb thing that happens in a relationship is bashing. This is when one person decides to trash the other person to family members, friends, coworkers, strangers…hell, essentially to anyone who will listen. This is beyond stupid. The main reason this is inane is because more often than not, you are going to stay with that person. Now, you have just created a vortex of hatred for your significant other. They are getting dirty looks at every family function because you ran your mouth about an argument that happened six months earlier.

You have to realize that every negative thing you say about your partner will be remembered by everyone. You may forgive him for cheating on you, but your best friend will never forgive him. Your mother or sister will never forgive him. They will remember that shit until the day they die and they will bring it up every time you mention his name. You could be talking about something as simple as, "Oh, he forgot to take out the trash this morning." They will respond with something like, "Well, he did cheat on you. You can't expect him to be responsible." Dear god, do not let this guy be late for something. All you will hear is, "He is probably out fucking that girl again."

Gentlemen, do not think this shit does not apply to you as well. Stop talking shit. Your friends will remember every detail. Without a doubt, your mom will bring it up 18 times per week.

Relationships are between those directly involved in them. A lot of relationships are harder than they need to be because they have become group activities. There are too many opinions. There are too many running mouths. Do not constantly promote negativity about your relationship unless you want to be in a relationship with 40 people.

An infinitely mind-boggling occurrence in relationships is the tendency to remain in relationships with people who are garbage. For the life of me, I will never understand why people stay with someone who makes them miserable. They hang on to people that they should leave. They stay in relationships that are clearly going nowhere because they assume they can make them work, with no evidence to support that assumption. As I said, some things are crazy. Some things are just plain stupid.

Political insanity:

The political stage is filled with an infinite number of examples of ridiculous behavior. Let me explain to you how politics works in this country. First, politics is like a religion for a lot of people. They have cult-like followings that believe anything and everything their party says. If anything goes wrong, they immediately blame the other side. Think about how God is never to blame- every evil is accounted for with Satan. Remove God and Satan and insert whatever political party fits your fancy. If you are a republican, it is never the fault of the Republican Party - the problem is 'those silly socialist democrats'. Similarly, if you identify yourself as a democrat, the blame falls squarely on the republicans. As I said, it is a cult-like following.

The method of shifting the blame works perfectly for the politicians. One, it is easier to make promises and not keep them. It is not your fault you have not done what you said you were going to do- those evil people on the other side hindered your progress. Two, and more importantly, it is easier for the government to divide the country. Republicans hate democrats and democrats hate republicans all across the nation. People loathe the other side. Everything is THEIR fault. Your country would be great if it was not for THEM!

Meanwhile, the upper echelons of government live like kings, making a ridiculous salary to work two days a week and accomplish nothing. They never represent the people because the people do not have enough money to pad the pockets of their elected officials. They can never represent the people because they do not understand the people. They look at people as a number, a statistic or a vote, never a human. How can you have the best interest of the people at heart when you have no idea what the people truly want, nor do you care to know?

You want to hear a fun fact? In the last 30 years, regardless of who has been in charge, the rich have gotten richer, the poor have gotten poorer. Regardless of whether the President was republican or democrat, the rich have gotten richer, the poor have gotten poorer. Regardless of whether Congress was controlled by Republicans or Democrats, the rich have excelled, the poor- not so much. Yet, there are many people who believe one side is for the rich and one side is for the poor. Well, if you look at the simple fact that under the control of both parties, the rich have always done well, it appears that no side is for the poor.

You want more insanity? A huge percentage of our voting populace does not vote for who they think would do the best job. They just vote against the person they feel will fuck up the most. It is amazing that our democratic process is not a selection of the best person for the job. It is an elimination process of people we do not want to run the country. After we go through the primaries, we get to choose between two people to be the President. Only two. There are over 315 million people in the United States, and we get to choose between two potential candidates. If you do not like either of the two, then tough shit- those are your choices. Some people wonder why there is a huge portion of our population that does not partake in the election process. It is because they feel the entire process is a joke and honestly, I cannot blame them for feeling that way.

Religion……… Oh Religion:

Where do I begin? There are so many stupid things that happen in the religious realm it is not even funny. I would like to stress that there are many religious folk who are sane and civil. In order to make my point about the problematic side of religion, I guess we can start with the extreme and the self-explanatory. If your god tells you that he wants you to blow yourself up and kill innocent people, tell him to do it first. If your god tells you to dance around with rattlesnakes to prove your worth, tell him to stop smoking whatever the fuck he is smoking. If your god wants you to drink from a cup of death, then drink up if you are that fucking stupid. If your god drills in your brain that you are better than everyone else for any reason, you and he are idiotic. Let's clear this up right now. You are not better than anyone. You are not selected. You are not the chosen one. You are a human, nothing more, nothing less. It does not matter how much crazy shit you do, it does not make you special.

Outside of the extreme, there are still a lot of idiotic things that occur within religion. You have people who are nobodies thinking they are somebodies, because they believe in a god. If you have no job, no money, a small amount of education, in a shitty marriage and everyone hates you, no amount of religion should ever make you feel important. People should want to do something more worthy in their life than just simply believing in a god.

One of the things that amaze me is how people let themselves get treated because of religion. In some religions, women are treated like animals. They are nothing more than breeding machines that are fenced into a house. Their entire existence, their entire purpose in life is to have children, care for the children, care for the husband and go to religious services. Now, if you choose this life because that is the life you want, then whatever - it is your life. If you were brainwashed into thinking that this is god's plan for your life, then you really need to wake the fuck up.

In some cases, animals are treated better than women. At least animals do not have to walk around, fully covered in the middle of summer because the other animals are not allowed to see them. In some religious societies, you would get in more trouble for beating or killing an animal than you would for beating or killing a woman. Again, this Church, my Church, is based on logic. Tell me, what kind of fucking logic is that and what sane person would ever want to be a part of that?

You want more stupidity? People pay a preacher or pastor 10% of their income because they believe that is what their god tells them to do. Throwing money at pastors apparently shows faithfulness to god. Preachers are famous for talking about paying your tithes to god and how if you want that new job or new car, you must remember to pay your tithes to the church.

Here is where logic comes in to play. An all-powerful god needs 10% of your check? A god that can create something out of nothing, that can heal the blind, raise the dead, part the sea, needs money? If god was so powerful, why can't he just give everything to his workers? I mean, he already owns everything, why does he need money? The even more fascinating thing is what happens to the money once it is collected. You have preachers that have million dollar houses, while their church members struggle to pay their rent. You have preachers with three or four cars, while their members catch the bus to church. You have preachers with thousand dollar suits and hundred dollar watches, while their members buy clothes of a discount rack at some low budget department store. Looking at this from a logical standpoint, you would scream "What the fuck are you guys thinking?" Then you realize the stupidity found in a brainwashed mind has no limits.

Religion also picks the dumbest fights in the world. You have a huge number of religious nuts fighting against homosexuals. Not just marriage – the whole demographic of gay people. They feel their lifestyle is evil, of Satan and I will use their word, an abomination. Interestingly enough, priests raping children gets brushed under the rug like nothing happened. You have assholes still fighting over whether or not god can be used or spoken about in schools. Oh, let us not worry about the fact that our children are dumb as a box of rocks. Look up the numbers for yourself. We rank far behind top countries in every major educational sector. In the educational war, we are getting our ass handed to us. Does that worry them? No, they have no time to worry about education being in our schools. They have to fight to make sure god is in our schools. They do not have time to worry about whether or not their child is actually learning something while they are in class for seven hours a day. They just want to make sure their child can say grace when they go to lunch.

Back to the whole homosexuality and marriage situation. Religious people have been fighting for years to stop homosexuals from getting married. They feel marriage is sacred and must be protected. This is the biggest fucking joke I have ever heard. They feel marriage is sacred? In a country where the divorce rate has been around 50% for years, marriage is sacred? In a world where some countries afford you the right to marry your rape victim, marriage is sacred? In a world where you can still get a wife for two goats and a couple of chickens, marriage is sacred? In a world where you can order a fucking wife through the mail or through a website, marriage is sacred? They are saying that bullshit because they do not like homosexuals. They do not give a damn about marriage or it being sacred. They just want to hold on to their "moral code" and their idiotic beliefs because it makes them feel better about themselves.

Speaking of moral code, the religious moral code is beyond stupid. You can kick an old lady down the stairs, punch a child in the face, steal money from a homeless person and kill a man for looking at you wrong and all you have to do is say, "Sorry god, my bad," and all is forgiven. You are a child of god and all your sins are washed away. If you raise orphan children, read to the elderly, work in a soup kitchen every weekend and give money to charity, but have a loving relationship with someone of the same sex, you are going to burn in hell forever. Apparently, god is more concerned with who is fucking who, than who is helping the citizens of this world live and be happy.

My problem is not the illogical thinking of their moral code. I know it is stupid. Anyone with a brain knows it is stupid. My problem is that they try to force the world to follow their moral code. My problem is they say stupid shit about their moral code like it is a fact. I had the misfortune of dealing with a number of religious people regarding moral code and religion. Many say that were there no religion in the United States, the country would collapse. Crime rates would go up. Divorce rates would go up. No one would do anything right or good because there would be no moral guidance that religion and god provide.

Obviously, I have had to call them out on their bullshit. I could not come at them in full force, seeing as it was not the proper setting for it. I did, however, kindly ask them what world they have been living in. I brought facts to the table, of course. I pointed out the fact that about 75% of all prison inmates identify themselves as Christians. Atheists actually make up less than 1% of the prison population. Atheist couples have a lower divorce rate than religious couples. I did not get a response, of course. I forgot when you bring logic and facts to an argument, the argument generally ends quickly.

I have had people tell me that we should look to religion for a proper moral code because godly people have a better moral code than atheists and/or non-believers. Okay, let's look into the religious moral code in question. Should atheists start strapping bombs to themselves and blowing people up? That is one religious moral code. Should agnostics start killing all the people who are not white? I mean, all white people are better than everyone else, right? Should they start lynching the niggers? Should they start burning crosses or shooting and killing those porch monkeys? That is another religious moral code. Should non-believers start telling people who live in countries that are infested with AIDS, to not wear condoms? Should they do everything in their power to hide and protect pedophiles? Should they go into poor neighborhoods and promise them a kingdom made of gold after they die, just to get their money? Should they marry six women and make them all live in a dungeon while they go out to find another wife?

I would love for a religious person to tell me exactly which moral code I am, or we are, supposed to follow. I do not believe in a god, yet I do not steal, kill or rape. I have never been to jail. I have gotten in a couple of fights in my life, but that is expected, right? Believe it or not, I try my hardest never to tell a lie. My motto is simple: if you do not want to hear the truth, do not ask me the question. I help those in the world around me that need help. I respect and love my wife, love my children, go to work every day and try my best to make the lives of those around me better. So, for all those that feel my moral code is not good because it does not include a god or some bullshit book - fuck you.

Living for the streets

This question is strictly for gang members. Let me get this straight. You guys are killing each other for some imaginary superiority over a piece of land that you motherfuckers do not even own? Can you please explain the logic in that? I understand that you may have had a rough life. Your parents may have been shitty. That still does not explain the logic in killing and dying for something that you will never possess. If you are doing it for money, there are easier ways to make money. If you are doing it for the thrill, get a better fucking hobby. In reality, no one cares if two gang bangers kill each other. If two idiots want to shoot it out because one is wearing red and the other is wearing blue, then have at it. The problem comes in when you non-aiming assholes shoot and kill innocent bystanders who have nothing to do with your asinine feud. Children are dying because you dumb fucks want to have shoot-outs in public places. I know this question will not help but I have to ask anyway, can you stop that shit?

Let me ask a question to all the people who like to live in the streets. Do you like sleeping with one eye open? Do you like leaving the house and being worried that someone is going to try and kill you? Do you like sitting on your couch and having to keep looking out of the window, paranoid that a drive-by could happen at any time? Do you like living with the fear that someone you love could be killed, at any moment, for something you did? If you answer 'no' to any of these questions, then it is time to pick a different life. If you answered yes to all of these questions, then you have clearly avoided common sense and logic throughout your life.

Ghetto Fantasies

I was going to start this section with something witty. I was going to start this section off nicely and then dive into what I wanted to say. Well, fuck all that. I have a question. Why are there so many people in the hood, in the ghetto, who only dream of being basketball players or rappers? It is ridiculous the amount of people who have the plan of being a rapper. What is even more ridiculous is that they always know somebody who knows somebody who is going to "put them on". Get the fuck out of here. Do not even get me started on all the future professional basketball players that live in the ghetto. When you ask them how they are going to make it, they all have the same answer. "I'm going to get a scholarship." The motherfucker cannot even spell scholarship, but he is going to get one.

Do not get me wrong. I do not knock people for having dreams. I do not knock people for chasing their dreams. What I think is stupid is when people have next to impossible dreams, yet fail to come up with a plan B. You can dream of being a professional football or basketball player, but what happens to you if you do not make it? Oh, and do not dare ask them that question. You will instantly be labeled a "hater" because you had the audacity to ask a logical question.

Another problem I have with ghetto fantasies is that they are always the same. They want to be professional players, rappers, video dancers, hair dressers, movie stars. All shit that requires little to no education. What happened to wanting to be a doctor or a lawyer? What happened to wanting to be a scientist or a teacher? What happened to wanting to do something that will actually make the world better?

Most ghetto fantasies are about getting rich. There are too many people in the ghetto trying to go straight from the outhouse to the penthouse. That explains why so many of them are trying to buy their way out of poverty. There was a study done about poor people and what they spent their money on. People, who make less than $13,000 a year, on average, spend $645 a year on lottery tickets. If you told these same people to put $500 per year in the bank to help themselves get on their feet, they would kindly remind you of how broke they are and how it is impossible for them to save money. There are too many people in poverty that are looking for the quick fix. The reason a lot of people never make it out of poverty is because the quick fix never comes.

Let's say you make it out, though. Let's say your fantasy comes true, then what? Do you have the intelligence to stay out of the ghetto? You may laugh at the question, but look at all the professional football players and basketball players who get the big paycheck and three years after they retire, they are broke. Look at all the lottery winners who are back in poverty five years after they win. The secret to escaping the ghetto is not money, it is education. You can have all the money in the world, but if you are not smart enough to know what to do with that money, you will be broke in no time. Pave your way to success with education and hard work. Keep your dreams, but do not forget to live in reality as well.

No good motherfuckers

Before I get to the stupid part, I have to talk about the fucked up part. There are men who feel they can sleep with a woman, get her pregnant, and then just bounce. What the hell kind of shit is that? Men, you have got to step up to the plate and take care of something you created. That is your child, your responsibility. I do not care if the mother is a bitch. I do not care if she is pulling every trick in the book to not let you see your children. I do not care if she is dumb, idiotic, a slut, a whore, a……..well, you get the point. First of all, you slept with her. So, you cannot blame anyone but yourself. Second of all, what does that have to do with the child? That child did not ask to be born. That child did not ask for the mother they got. Regardless of how the mother is, you owe that child your time, your efforts, your life. That does not change just because you do not like the mother.

Now that I have gotten the fucked up part out of the way, on to the stupid shit. One of the things I find funny about some of these vanishing fathers, is that they get extremely upset when they find out their child is calling another man "daddy". They get pissed. They say stupid shit like, "I'm her father. She ain't calling another man daddy. I'll kill that motherfucker, for real!" Really? Now you want to play daddy? You have not seen your child in 5 years. The last time you saw her was on accident. You just ran into her at a store.

You smiled at her, gave her five dollars, promised to call her and went on your merry way. She has not heard from you since. Another man has stepped up and performed the task which you failed to do, and you want to get angry? You really need to grow the fuck up.

You want to know how to prevent something like this from happening? Be your child's father. You fight for your child. You fight to see your child. You show your child that you love them more than anything in the world. You make sacrifices for your child. You try your hardest to be everything your child could ever want in a father. So, if the mother does come around with another man and says to them, "This is your new daddy." Your child will quickly say, "That is not my daddy and he never will be my daddy."

One more funny thing about no good motherfuckers. Is it me, or do these no good fathers always seem to come out of nowhere when their child becomes famous or rich? If their child was a manager of a convenience store, they would never try to find them. As soon as they see their child with a professional team or something similarly high-profile, they are on television doing interviews on how they miss their baby and just want to be a part of their life. Get the fuck out of here. When it was time to buy diapers, your ass disappeared quickly. When it was time to buy milk and clothes, no one could find you. When it was time to support their dreams, you were out of sight. Now that your child has become successful, you want to appear on the scene like nothing happened. When your child needed you to take care of them, you said, "Fuck you". Now that you want your child to take care of you, they say, "Fuck you." It is called Karma bitch, and you were just smacked with it.

Risk takers

There are a number of people that risk their lives in the most idiotic ways possible. I am not talking about the people who sky dive or swim with sharks or things like that. Though you may consider that stupid, generally those people are around professionals and there is a certain level of safety. Now, if you and a group of friends decided to just jump in an ocean full of sharks, then you would be considered stupid.

What I am talking about are the people that risk their lives on a daily basis for no reason other than being dumb. We see people like this every day, especially if you drive anywhere. There is always some dumbass on the road going fifty miles an hour, talking on the phone, smoking a cigarette and trying to adjust the radio. It amazes me how many people get behind the wheel and feel they do not have to pay attention to the road. We have all seen the commercials or heard the stories of people who died because they were texting while driving. It is quite simple. If one mistake can kill you, you might want to pay attention.

There are other people that do stupid shit as well. I have had this argument plenty of times with women. Yes, you should be allowed to wear whatever it is that you want to wear, but that does not mean it is safe to wear it. If you walk into a club with a skirt barely below your ass and a shirt just big enough to cover your nipples, you are going to draw attention from a lot of guys. The problem for you is you may draw attention from a lot of guys that have no problem raping a woman. Now, I would never blame the victim for getting raped or assaulted. In an ideal world, a woman can walk into a place ass naked and would not have to fear for her life or safety. Unfortunately, we do not live in an ideal world. We live in a very sick world and you should take that into account before you walk out of the door. I understand that you may want to look cute, but your safety should be far more important to you than your looks.

Self Esteem

There are different levels of self-esteem. You may have low self-esteem where you feel you are undeserving of praise or have a feeling of worthlessness. You feel your life has no value whatsoever and most times, you just float through life, unwilling to really commit yourself to anything of consequence. High self-esteem can vary. Someone can have a healthy self-esteem or a self-esteem that makes them an arrogant jackass. You have to find a balance within yourself to have a good, solid self-esteem.

Proceeding to the idiotic shit when it comes to self-esteem... Some people have a high self-esteem for no logical reason. If you are an ass, broke, fat and ugly, you have no right to be arrogant. If you are dumb as a box of rocks, you have no right to be arrogant. I generally do not mind people having a high self-worth. In fact, I encourage it. What I do have a problem with are people who act like they are better than other people. Have you ever met an ugly arrogant person? It is the most confusing and frustrating situation in the world. You look at them with pity and disbelief. You cannot figure out how someone who looks so bad, thinks they are better than anyone. As I said, I do not mind someone having confidence in themselves. I want you to feel you are worth something. I want you to believe in yourself. Just do not allow that confidence to turn into arrogance.

Low self-esteem is very tricky. I really should not come down on people hard because it could destroy their psyche. Then again, when have I ever held back? Low self-esteem is usually a product of horrible parents, horrible friends, a horrible spouse or just a horrible living situation. A lot of people only hear negative shit in their life and they take it to heart. Then again, it is hard to fault them in some situations. If you have been hearing that "you are a piece of shit" since you were two years old, it might be hard not to believe.

What I will tell those with low self-esteem is to stop listening to people. If any friend or family member makes you feel like shit - then to hell with them. I will never understand why people continue to deal with people that make them feel low or worthless. If you are a child with parents who do it, hang in there until you can take care of yourself and get the fuck away at the first opportunity. I am not telling you to run away. I am telling you to turn 18 and bounce as fast as you can. If you can go to a safe place before you get of age and live, a safe relative's house for example, then go. There should be no room in your life for people who try to mentally destroy you.

If you are an adult, what in the hell is your problem? Grow a fucking backbone, put those assholes in their place and remove them from your life, immediately. You have nothing holding you back, except yourself.

One of the things I find truly fascinating is how someone's self-esteem can change. If a spouse or loved one says something like, "You are fat" or "You are ugly", their self-esteem goes through the floor. They feel sad and depressed. If a stranger were to say it, some people's self-esteem would drop, but most would just blow it off as the stranger is a fucking jerk. Now, if a spouse or loved one were to say "You are beautiful", generally, it would have no effect on the average person. If a stranger were to say the same thing, their self-esteem would go through the roof. How fucking psychotic is that?

People are conditioned to never believe positive things that come from loved ones because they believe loved ones are merely playing the role. My personal favorite is, "You are just saying that to be nice." If you were to say something negative, they take it to heart immediately. That is where low self-esteem pisses me off. You project your low self-worth onto the ones that are closest to you. A lot of times, they have nothing to do with your mental problems. They just decided to love you and be there for you, yet you hold them hostage with your insecurities.

As nicely as I can say this, you have got to find some value in your life. You have got to focus on your positive attributes. If you only dwell on what you do not have, what you cannot do, how you do not look - it makes you a negative person. You project that negativity onto other people. Then, you wonder why you cannot find any good friends or a good person to share your life with. If you do not like yourself, why in the hell would anyone else like you?

Drama Queens

If you could not tell by now, I hate drama queens. I touched on this a little earlier in Job, but now I really want to go after these assholes. There are different types of drama queens. Some want to start trouble all the time. Then, there are drama queens that always find a reason to be depressed and apocalyptic. The type I specifically want to discuss is the latter.

Oh how I hate the depressed drama queen. These are the people who live a life where apparently nothing goes right. They are the ones where if it could happen, it does happen, to them. Here is my problem with them – they constantly need to exaggerate just how bad things really are to get attention. They will blow up a story to make it seem like it was such a horrible event, when in reality, it was not.

I will give you an example. Take a situation where someone gets a flat tire. A typical person may tell the story as such:

Man, I was driving home from the store and my tire blew out. I had to wait for the tow truck to get there and change the tire because I could not get it off. I got home late because it took him a while to get there so I did not have time to cook dinner. We ordered Chinese food and just relaxed and watched a movie. Besides my tire going flat and scaring the shit out of me, I had a pretty good night.

Now, the exact same story told from someone who is a drama queen:

Oh my god, I had a horrible night. I was driving and my tire exploded. I almost hit three cars. I was able to get to the side of the road, but just barely. The tow truck driver took forever. I got home late and could not even cook dinner. We had to order Chinese because that is what the kids wanted. I hate Chinese and they know I hate Chinese, but I got it anyway. Then I had to watch this stupid ass movie. My neighbor came over and looked at my car and he said it looks like I damaged my engine when my tire exploded. It is going to be like $3000 to fix it. And you know I do not have that kind of money because I've been a little sick – I probably have cancer.

I am going to stop there, because that story can go on and on. Anyone who has ever had the pleasure of dealing with a drama queen knows that this is a 3 hour event. You will get phone calls, e-mails and emergency face to face sessions with this person about this event. You will hear about this story until the next life threatening / altering event happens. Then they will go on to the next event and drill that into the head of anyone who is willing to listen. They will bring it up regardless of who they are talking to. Some random person could walk past and ask a simple question like, "How are you doing?" Without a doubt they will reference their brush with death in their answer, "Well, I almost got into an accident that could have killed me when my tire exploded, but I am fine now." The worst possible thing that someone could ask a drama queen is, "What happened?" You better get comfortable. You are in for a long story.

The problem with people like this is that they burden the world around them with their bullshit. They seek attention by trying to make people feel sorry for them. It is childish.

For those that say, "Well, you don't know my life. I do not exaggerate how bad it is. It really is that bad," Then change your fucking life. I hate people that complain and bitch about their life and do nothing to change it. If your life is as bad as you say it is, then do something to fix it. If you do not want to, then please shut the fuck up about it.

For the drama queens that like to start trouble, please get a fucking life. That is all.

Is it a child or not?

One of the dumbest things that happen in this nation is that we have selective definitions of age. By this I mean that one day a person is considered a child. The next day that person could be considered an adult. Generally, this happens when the law is trying to fuck someone, royally, so they conveniently change what a person is considered. Let me explain this further.

If a fourteen year old girl sleeps with a twenty year old man and the police find out about it, then that girl is considered a child and that man is going to get locked up for having sex with a minor. She is a child and how dare that man have sex with a child. She could not make a reasonable decision to sleep with that man. She does not understand the consequences of her actions because she is only fourteen. They will say that man preyed upon her because she was young and gullible. They will say that she did not know any better. She is impressionable and easily manipulated. Essentially she is a child.

If that same fourteen year old girl were to kill a twenty year old man and the police find out about it, then that girl is considered an adult in the eyes of the law. She knew exactly what she was doing. She knew the consequences of her actions and she knew that what she was doing was wrong. She made the adult decision to kill a man in cold blood. She should not be looked at as a child. She should be viewed as the killer that she is and they will lock her up in prison for as many years as possible (anywhere from 20 years to life).

I should not have to say this because I am more than sure you get the point I am trying to make, but I will say it anyway. What the fuck kind of logic is this? So, if a teenager kills someone, then they are an adult. If a teenager sleeps with an adult, they are a child? How in the hell can this pass for law?

Now, I am not saying that a thirteen year old should be allowed to sleep with a thirty year old. What I am saying is that the law should have some kind of consistency when dealing with teenagers. How can they be considered a child in a statutory rape case but an adult in a murder case or in any other case? It seems to be that this country is quick to lock up anyone they can and they do not care if they have to change definitions to accomplish it.

Make it count

We have all heard stories of stupid criminals. My personal favorite is about a guy who decided to rob a bank. He wrote "Give me all your money" or something to that effect on the back of a piece of paper and gave it to the teller. He got the money and left the bank. The only problem with this criminal mastermind plan was that he wrote it on the back of his paystub. It had his name, address, social security number, everything. You want to talk about a short investigation. I also love the stories of people who steal shit and put it up on the internet for sell. Do they not know they can trace that auction right back to them?

I was going to do a "How to be a Criminal" section, but I do not think it would be a good idea. I will, however, tell you two rules that any criminal should follow. One, always work alone. The main reason is that you will not tell on yourself. Well, unless you are an idiot. If you are, then you deserve to be caught. Two, make whatever crime you are doing, count. I will never understand why people rob places like convenient stores or gas stations. If you get caught, you are doing at least five to ten years and at the most, you get $100. To me, that is not worth it. Generally, in the best possible situation you are getting $20 a year for your crime. In no realm of reality is that a crime worth committing.

Before anyone gets confused, I am not a criminal nor do I plan to be. There is no amount of money that is worth being separated from my children. I also know that I would make a horrible criminal. I am too paranoid. I would always think someone is following me. I would check the mirror everyday just to make sure the guy staring back at me did not have plans to screw me over. As I said, I am way too paranoid to be a criminal.

That being said, some people need to realize that criminal activity is not for them. If you have been to jail three or four times, then maybe you need to pick a new line of work. Clearly you are not smart enough to commit a crime and not get caught. Do you not think it is time to reevaluate your career path? If not, then continue to do stupid shit and get caught. At least it will give the rest of us something to laugh at when you get busted, again.

Fucking Drive

I think I could just say the title and everyone will understand the gist of this section. The amount of stupid shit that people do while driving is amazing. A number of things that people do while driving blow my mind. A lady got in a car accident because she was driving while trying to shave her lower region. A man got into a car accident because he was watching porn while driving. While those stories are a show of extreme stupidity, many drivers do things that are still stupid, just not quite that stupid.

The first thing I want to say is please pay attention while you are operating a motor vehicle. Nothing angers me more than to be on the road with drivers that seem to be doing everything but driving. Here is a quick list of some of the shit I have observed other drivers doing while driving:

- The most obvious is that everyone is on their cell phone. Get off the fucking phone and drive. This includes texting as well. Please put your phone away an pay attention to the fucking road

- Drivers having a picnic in their car. I do not mind someone eating a sandwich or whatever while driving. I do mind someone having a buffet in their front seat or a big ass bowl of something sitting on the steering wheel. If your hands are on the bowl and your eyes are in the bowl, who is driving the fucking car?

- Drivers shaving. So, you really think it is smart to have a razor by your throat while going 60 miles per hour? Interesting.

- Drivers sitting at a green light. Green means go! Either you are not paying attention or you are color blind. Either way, get your ass out of the way.

- Drivers beating their children. I understand that children need discipline. I do not understand disciplining your child while driving down the road. I have seen drivers turned completely around while screaming or hitting their child. If you are looking in the back seat and your child is in the back seat, who is watching the road?

- Drivers just stopping. This usually happens when the genius behind the wheel realizes that he or she is about to miss their exit on the highway. So, instead of just taking the next exit and doubling back, this special kind of asshole decides to simply stop in the middle of the highway and wait to get over. This is extremely dangerous, but that is of no concern. They cannot miss their exit!

- Nosy ass drivers. Apparently, if there is an accident, a car pulled over by a cop, a car broken down or just a person walking, every driver that rides past must go 2 miles per hour to make sure they see everything that is going on. For the love of beans, move your punk ass on. If you really must see what is going on, pull over to the side of the road. Either way, get the fuck out of the way. I have witnessed a driver crash into the back of another driver because he was busy looking at another accident. I think that says it all.

- Drivers multitasking. These are the idiots that are on the cell phone and computer while driving. Or they are eating, smoking and talking on the phone. These are the people that feel they need to do twelve other things while driving. Needless to say, they are a pain in the ass to share the road with.

There are other things that drivers do that make me crazy. One of the most annoying things in the world is to be stuck behind a driver going 30 miles per hour, but as soon as the light changes to yellow, this son of a bitch wants to speed up to make the light. Sometimes they even run a red light! Can we all agree that when someone does this shit, it should be legal to chase them down and punch them in the fucking face? Another thing - when drivers decide to jump in front of you going 30 miles per hour when you are doing 60. That shit deserves a punch in the face as well.

I could go on and on, but I will wrap it up with this. If you are on the road, please pay attention to what you are doing and drive. If you do not know how to drive, then get the fuck off the road.

Man Section
(Asshole time)

How to cheat and not get caught

There are rules to cheating. If you do not believe me, look at all the people who have broken these simple rules and been caught. If you do not want to be like one of those dumb asses, you should keep reading. Please note, I am not saying that it is okay to cheat, but if you are going to cheat, you should at least do it right. Before I get into the complex rules, I will get the obvious ones out of the way. Those rules are as follows:

Never save anything – No e-mails, pictures, text messages, voicemails, letters, etc. You never want to leave any kind of evidence that could be found.

Never cheat with an ugly chick – I mean, what is the fucking point?

Never mess with a psycho chick – If you do not know why, then you should not be cheating in the first place.

Never cheat with a neighbor – Or anyone in your neighborhood. Though it may be convenient, it is too close to home.

Never fall in love – Feelings should never get involved when you are cheating. If they do, then you need to end it immediately.

Never run your mouth – The more people that knows what you are doing, the more likely you will get caught.

Never tell a ridiculous lie – If you have to lie, keep it short, sweet and simple. Do not put a lot of details in the lie. Also, if you are going to include others in your lie, make sure they know they were included.

Never have a second relationship – If you find yourself arguing with your side chick, then it is time to cut her off. She is there for fun, not drama.

Those are the simple rules. If you follow those, you are on the path to being a successful cheater. If you really want to be master, you will follow these rules.

Always tell the truth – The best way to cover your tracks is to always have some truth in your story. If you go to the store to meet your side chick, then tell your girl you went to the store. You obviously will leave out the part where she blew you in the parking lot. You just say, "I went to the store" and you are good. Main reason this works is because you do not have to try and remember a lie. You really did go to the store. A lot of people get caught because they say one thing and then three weeks later they say something completely different. If you tell the truth while leaving out minor details, you will never get caught in a lie. Also, if you want to help your case, buy something at the store. It makes your story that much more believable.

Never change – The reason some people get caught is because they become a completely different person when they start cheating. They start shaving more or dressing differently. They work-out more or wear different cologne. You cannot change the person you are just because you are getting some on the side. The worst thing you could possibly do while cheating is to start acting differently. That sends an immediate signal to your wife or girlfriend that something is going on. Stay the same or risk getting busted.

Be honest – I know some of you may think I am crazy, but this if the best advice I could give you. If you are trying to get a girl to be your side piece, you better make sure she knows she is the side piece. The last thing you need in your life is another girl that expects to be number one. I understand that it may be harder to get a girl to accept the side girl role, especially one that is not ugly, but it is worth it if you can.

Devise a schedule – The reason being honest is so important is because it allows you to create a schedule that both of you will follow. If she thinks she is number one, she will have no reservations about calling you at three o'clock in the morning. I do not care how good you are, it is hard to explain to your main girl why this chick is calling you all hours of the night. Being honest makes it easy for you to create a plan on when you two will talk, text and meet up. You can avoid the middle of the night phone calls and also avoid her getting mad at you for not responding when she calls or texts. More importantly, it will make sure your home life is not interrupted by some unwanted communication attempt.

Get a girl with something to lose – Your side girl has to have something to lose if she gets caught. If she is free to fuck up your life, without the possibility of fucking up hers, you are at her mercy. If she has just as much to lose if she gets caught, then she will be just as careful as you are. She will not call you in the middle of the night because her husband is at home and that will fuck up her home life. She will not demand more of your time because she has other things to do than to sit at home and wait on you. She does not have time to invade your house. She will be busy making sure her house is not getting invaded.

Introduce the girl into your life – This is only for the expert cheaters. If you are good enough, you can bring up your side chick in random conversations to get your main girl used to the name. Some people may think it is crazy, but if executed correctly, it will make your life so much easier. You can introduce her as a friend or co-worker. Here is the key. Do not bring her up too much and it is best to mention her in a problem. Say something like, "I was talking to Tiffany today, my co-worker, and she was asking me questions about marriage. Apparently, she is having problems with her husband and needed someone to talk to." It makes you look like the sensitive, caring person and it puts her name out there. So, if there ever comes a time when Tiffany does call while your wife is home, you can easily play it off like, "Oh, she must want to talk about her husband." You have a brief conversation and get off the phone. Again, the key is to not to do it too much.

Know when you cut loose – Sometimes you just have to let the side girl go. If you or her are catching feelings, then it is time to call it quits. If you or her are feeling too much heat at home, then it is time to call it quits. If she is calling too much or becoming too clingy, you have to cut her off. You have to know when to abort mission. Regardless of how good she is or how great your situation is, sometimes you just have to end it.

If you follow these simple rules, you should be successful at cheating. There are different rules for women but I refuse to say them. You want to know why, because I will not help women cheat. Fucking whores!

(For women) How to make your man happy

Shut…..the…..fuck……up.

How to win an argument

When arguing with a woman you need to remember a number of things. Sadly, most men do not understand how to argue with a woman. That is what I am here for. I will give you all the tools you need to win any argument with any woman. Well, you may not win every argument, but you will definitely hold your own. The rules are simple to understand and I am writing this so that you can read it as much as you need to.

1. **Know why you are arguing**. Too many times men get caught up in an argument and they have no idea why they are arguing. Sometimes, women just want to argue about something. Sometimes,

women have something on their mind and they want to argue to see how you react. Sometimes, women are mad at something else and they just want to argue with you because they cannot argue with the person they are mad at. I must say, sometimes you fuck up and they are going to let you have it. Before you engage in an argument, you first need to realize why you are arguing.

2. **Know what you are arguing about**. Have you ever been in an argument and you are winning, then magically the argument changes and you are getting your ass handed to you? This is called "The Switch". When a woman is losing an argument, she often changes the argument to something that she can win. You will start off arguing about her spending too much money and before you know it, you are talking about something that happened fifteen years ago with some girl named Tiffany (Apparently, Tiffany is a fucking slut). Remember to stick to what you are arguing about. She will flip that shit on you in a heartbeat.

3. **Know where you are arguing**. If you are at her mother's house or in front of her friends, do not argue. It is not worth it and you will never win. Even if you win, you will lose because you will then have an argument about how you embarrassed her in front of her family and/or friends. If you are in a restaurant and she likes to get loud, do not

argue with her. It is not worth the insanity that will ensue from you two arguing. Again, it is important to know where you are arguing.

4. **Know who you are arguing with**. If you have to sleep with that woman at night, you might not want to call her a dumb, fat bitch. If that woman is your boss, you might want to hold back on some of the things you want to say. You cannot argue with every woman the same way. You cannot argue with your sister the same way you argue with your grandmother. Know who you are arguing with and adjust your strategy.

The point of this chapter is to help men in arguments. Here is a list of some things that you need to know when arguing:

- Know what you are going to say. Do not just talk to talk.
- Know when to get out of an argument.
- Do not weaken because she cries. That is a woman's defensive move.
- If you are wrong, you have to admit it.
- You are not always right, but then again, neither is she.

There is one thing that I have to stress before I end this chapter. Do not be the first to drop the bomb. There is a point in every argument where you feel like you want to just lay down the hammer. Before you go Hiroshima on her ass, you need to remember that once you do, there is no coming back. Once you say whatever it is that you are dying to say, your relationship will never be the same. You have to allow her to strike the first death strike, and then you destroy her ass. You cannot be the first to do it because that means you are just a fucking jerk. If you do it in retaliation, then you cannot be at fault.

How to train your wife

I personally am fond of the good old back hand. It is reliable and easily accessible. Once you do it a couple of times, all you have to do is raise your hand and she knows. It reminds me of a joke I once heard, "What do you tell a woman with two black eyes? Nothing. She has already been told twice."

Okay, in all seriousness, there are easy ways to train your wife. If she is around you too much, you can say in a very sweet and loving voice, "Baby, I cannot miss you if you do not leave." Or, you can remind her that the kitchen is her natural habitat. If she needs help, start putting her make-up next to the pots and pans. Remind her how sexy she looks with a sandwich in one hand and a glass of something in the other. Stress to her that her mouth is not for talking, but for other things. Well, you can allow her to talk when it is necessary. I mean, how else will she know what you want on your sandwich if she cannot ask you?

For all the women who are reading this with their man and have something to say about this chapter, can I remind you of one thing? We told you to shut the fuck up two chapters ago. You should not be speaking right now. Kind sir, you may put the book down now and handle that situation. Do not be too mad at her though. Remember, she is only a woman.

How to win a fist fight

I want to explain that there are two different types of fist fights. There is one where you get into an altercation with a friend and one where you get into an altercation with an enemy. I will cover the friend one first.

There will be some people who do not understand why friends fight. As with any relationship, there are going to be ups and downs. You may come to a point in a friendship where a person says or does something that causes fists to fly. If this happens, just keep in mind that you guys are still friends. You can throw punches, but keep it to just that. No weapons should be used in the fight. Knock him on his ass, but do not try to injure or kill him. Do not try to break bones or permanently damage him, just let him know you are not to be fucked with. After the fight is over, the problem should go away and you can move on with life. Do not let a pointless argument or disagreement end a true friendship.

If the person is an enemy, then all bets are off. The first rule in fighting an enemy is there are no rules in fighting an enemy. You beat the living hell out of them and you do not stop until you feel safe. You use anything you need to. As I said, there are no rules.

Now that the rules are out of the way, let's get to how you win a fist fight. First of all, you have to know that about 90% of the people in this world cannot fight worth shit. They just throw punches wildly and hope for the best. When the punches do not land, they grab on to you and hold on for dear life. Most people punch themselves out in the first minute of a fight. They get tired and weak. You can use this to your advantage. Keep moving and picking your spots. Do not throw punches wildly, but aim your punches and make them count.

Another thing you need to remember is that most people get scared to death when they fight. Most people naturally get afraid when confronted with violence. Do not think you are a weak person because you feel fear. Fear just means you are human. Do not let the fear control you. Keep your mind clear, keep your thoughts on your opponent and remain aware of everything that is going on around you.

Last thing, you may run across one of the few people in this world that can fight their ass off. You may get your ass whooped. You may get knocked out. If you do, that is okay. It is not the end of the world - everyone catches an ass whooping at least once in their life. Just learn from what you did wrong and you will be fine.

How to deal with bullies

This is mainly for what you should tell your children. If your son or daughter has an asshole child at school picking on them, then tell your child to either ignore them or teach them some jokes to respond with. It sucks to be the butt of countless jokes. The only way for them to really defend themselves is to joke back. Remember, sticks and stones..... There is no point in having your child respond in a violent way to a couple of jokes.

If your child has another child or children at school putting their hands on them, then the whole ballgame changes. You need to explain to your child that they should punch that other child in the fucking face, and they do not stop until a teacher pulls them off. Understand that your child will be afraid. They will be scared of getting into trouble or getting punched back. You need to alleviate those fears. Explain to them that they are living in fear anyway. Explain to them that if they want that fear to stop, they have to stand up for themselves. Even if they get their ass whooped, they have to stand up for themselves. Explain that the bully will not stop until they make them stop.

If there are a group of bullies (sometimes, these bitch ass bullies travel in packs) tell your child to pick up a chair or a book and smack the fuck out of them. Again, do not stop until the teacher pulls them off. They have to go crazy. They have to plan it out. All they need to do is catch one of them at a time. They cannot be in a group all day, every day. Catch one of them in the bathroom by themselves and try to rip their fucking face off. I promise you, after your son or daughter attacks them enough times, they will leave them alone.

Some people may frown at this section. They may say I am being too hostile towards children. Let me explain something real fast. I hate bullies. I hate people that attack or pick on those that may be weaker than them. I feel that no mercy should be shown towards those assholes.

Another thing, I would rather a child punch a bully in the face than to bring a gun to school and shoot them. I would rather a child get into a couple of fights and have a couple of bruises, than for them to feel their situation is hopeless and they take their own life. There have been a number of children who have killed themselves over bullying. No parent should ever have to bury their child. If it came down to either a fight or a funeral, I am pretty sure all parents would take a fight any day of the week and twice on Sundays.

Closing Remarks

This is my asshole chapter. Anyone who knows me knows that I joke like this. Please know that I would never advocate violence against women. It should not need to be said that I respect women. I know that women play an important role in our society. I mean, food does not make itself! Hey, surely you know a bible would not be a bible if it did not make women feel belittled and worthless!

Contradictions in the Christian Bible

This chapter is dedicated to all the contradictions found in the Christian Bible. Before I start, I want to quote a verse from the Christian Bible:

Revelation, Chapter 22:18-19 – And I solemnly declare to everyone who reads this book: If anyone adds anything to what is written here, God shall add to him the plagues described in this book. And if anyone subtracts any part of these prophecies, God shall take away his share in the Tree of Life, and in the Holy City just described.

So, according to the Christian Bible, we are not supposed to add or take anything away from the book. Essentially, we cannot change the text in any way. We must take the bible as complete and whole. It can be argued that the author of Revelation was saying this about his book specifically, but that would be a pretty weak argument.

Now that we have established that we cannot add or subtract any words to or from the bible, we move on to the contradictions.

Genesis, Chapter 1 – God created plants, then animals, then man, then woman.

Genesis, Chapter2 – God created man, then plants, then animals, then woman.

Shit, we could not get past page 2 of the Christian bible before we found a contradiction.

Exodus, 9:1-7 – "Go back to Pharaoh," the Lord commanded Moses, "and tell him, 'Jehovah the God of the Hebrews, demands that you let his people go to sacrifice to him. If you refuse, the power of God will send a deadly plague to destroy your cattle, horses, donkeys, camels, flocks and herds. But the plague will affect only the cattle of Egypt; none of the Israeli herds and flocks will be touched.

The Lord announced that the plague would begin the very next day, and it did. The next morning all the cattle of the Egyptians began dying, but not one of the Israeli cattle were dead, yet when he found out that it was so, even then his mind remained unchanged and he refused to let the people go.

Exodus 9:18-20 – "Well, tomorrow about this time I will send a hailstorm across the nation such as there has never been since Egypt was founded. Quick! Bring in your cattle from the fields, for every man and animal left out in the fields will die beneath the hail!"

Some of the Egyptians, terrified by this threat, brought their cattle and slaves in from the fields.

Hmmmm, what fucking cattle are they talking about? You mean the cattle that were already destroyed in the plague that came before the hailstorm? Here is a quick explanation of what happened. God sent a plague to kill all the animals of Egypt. Then, the very next plague, he sent a hailstorm to hit Egypt and killed anything left outside, including the cattle of the Egyptians. So, again, I ask, what fucking cattle? Supposedly, he already killed them all. The only way for this story to make sense is for the Egyptians to have had backup cattle that god knew nothing about. They could have stolen cattle from the Israelis, but the Christian bible does not mention anything about that and we are not allowed to add anything to the stories. They could have brought more cattle, but again, that would be adding to the story. As the story reads, god killed all the cattle and turned right around and threatened to kill all the cattle again. Unless god has dementia, this story makes no sense.

2 Samuel 24:8-9 – Having gone through the entire land, they completed their task in nine months and twenty days. And Joab reported the number of the people to the king – 800,000 men of conscription age in Israel, and 500,000 in Judah

2 Samuel 24:17-18 – When David saw the angel, he said to the Lord, "Look, I am the one who has sinned! What have these sheep done? Let your anger be only against me and my family."

That day Gad came to David and said to him, "Go and build an altar to the Lord on the threshing floor of Araunah the Jebusite."

1 Chronicles 21:4-5 – But the king won the argument, and Joab did as he was told; he traveled all through Israel and returned to Jerusalem. The total population figure which he gave came to 1,100,000 men of military age in Israel and 470,000 in Judah.

1 Chronicles 21:17-18 – And David said to God, "I am the one who sinned by ordering the census. But what have these sheep done? O Lord my God, destroy me and my family, but do not destroy your people."

Then the angel of the Lord told Gad to instruct David to build an altar to the Lord at the threshing-floor of Ornan the Jebusite.

There are a number of problems with this story. It is a repetition of the story about a census that David took, but as you can see, there are contradictions within the stories. First, the numbers do not match. In 2 Samuel, you have 800,000 men Israel, 500,000 in Judah. In 1 Chronicles, you have 1,100,000 men in Israel and 470,000 in Judah. Now, I have heard that Samuel is breaking down the total and 1 Chronicles is providing the grand total of Israel, but also providing the total of Judah. The only problem with that logic is that the numbers do not add up. The total in 2 Samuel is 1,300,000. The total in 1 Chronicles is 1,100,000. That's a 200,000 difference. Regardless of how your try to make sense of the numbers, they simply do not add up. That is a big problem in a book that is supposed to be the holy of holies.

The second problem is where David is supposed to build the altar. In 2 Samuel, it is Araunah's threshold. In 1 Chronicles, it is Ornan's threshold. Can we at least get the person's name right?

There is also another contradiction in this story. The punishment choices that god gave David. In 2 Samuel, the choices are 7 years of famine, 3 months of fleeing from your enemies or 3 days of plague. In 1 Chronicles, the choices are 3 years of famine, 3 months of destruction by the enemies of Israel or 3 days of plague.

Matthew 27:5-8 – Then he threw the money onto the floor of the Temple and went out and hanged himself. The chief priests picked the money up. "We can't put it in the collection," they said, "since it's against our laws to accept money paid for murder."

They talked it over and finally decided to buy a certain field where the clay was used by potters, and to make it into a cemetery for foreigners who died in Jerusalem. That is why the cemetery is still called "The Field of Blood."

Acts 1:17-19 – Judas was one of us, chosen to be an apostle just as we were. He brought a field with the money he received for his treachery and falling headlong there, he burst open, spilling out his bowels. The news of his death spread rapidly among all the people of Jerusalem, and they named the place 'The Field of Blood.'

This one is obvious. How did Judas really die? Did he hang himself or just fall headlong in a field and explode? Who brought the field, the priests or Judas? Is it 'The Field of Blood' because of Judas' death or because it is the location of burial for foreigners?

Another huge contradiction is at the end of Matthew, Mark, Luke and John. If you read Matthew, chapters 27 – 28, Mark, chapters 15-16, Luke, chapters 23-24 and John, chapters 18-20, you will see what I am talking about. In short, they are all talking about the time from when Jesus stood before Pilate, all the way to his death and resurrection. This should not surprise you- they are different. Some of the differences are small. Some of them are really huge and potentially alter the entire story. In Matthew, Mark and Luke - Jesus said next to nothing to Pilate. In John, Jesus would not shut up. With regard to Jesus' death, Mark's description is of Jesus feeling scared and alone. John's description is of Jesus feeling confident and in charge. There are many other contradictions in this section. What Jesus says at his death changes from book to book. What happens at the tomb on the Sunday following his death changes from book to book.

There are a lot of contradictions when it comes to numbers. You can look at 1 Kings, 4:26 and 2 Chronicles 9:25 as examples of this. 1 Kings says Solomon had forty thousand chariot horses and employed twelve thousand charioteers. 2 Chronicles says Solomon had 4,000 stalls of horses and chariots, and 12,000 cavalrymen. Well, at least they got one number right.

There are many, many more contradictions, but I am not going to write them all. There are a number of websites that have them listed, though some of them are hard to follow. If you are arguing with a person about the contradictions, I have provided you with more than enough ammunition to win that argument, hands down. I must warn you though, speaking logic to someone who has been brainwashed into thinking the Christian Bible is infallible is a long and frustrating task. If you are going to do it, good luck.

Every time there is a duplicate story in the Bible, contradictions seem to incur. If this book was truly inspired by an all knowing, all powerful god, you would think he would not get confused about details of the stories.

Counter Arguments

Abortions

There are a number of things I want to tackle when it comes to arguments about abortion. The first one I want to talk about is "A woman's right to choose". My argument is not that a woman should not have a right to choose. I just want to know where is the man's right to choose? What choice does a man get besides when he wants to pay child support? How in the world did we ever come to a place in this society where only women get to choose whether or not a child is born? Technically, it is the man's child as well. Should he not get a say on whether or not his unborn child is terminated?

It is amazing to me how if a woman wants the baby and the man does not, he is not being responsible. If a man wants the baby and the woman does not, he is just screwed. To make this situation fair, there has to be some change. I would never advocate for a man to force a woman to have a baby she does not want. What I would push for is for men to have the right to wash their hands of a child, just like a woman can. I know this sounds fucked up and I know some people will say, "Well, men are doing that already." While that is true, women can still take that man to court and get child support, label him as a no-good father, etc. Some women hope to get pregnant so that they can take the man to court and get child support. I hope you did not think all those women sleep with famous people just to say they slept with them. A number of them hope to get pregnant so that they can get ten thousand dollars a month in child support. Apparently, their child needs gold pampers or some shit. Women get a way out if they do not want a baby. Men have no such option. Women get a choice. Men get responsibility. Women fought for years to make everything equal. Well, this certainly is not equal. Let's go women. You have more fighting to do.

The next argument is the whole, "Well, we need abortions for all those women who get pregnant from rape or incest." I agree, abortion should be there for those cases, but that is not the reason that the majority of abortions take place. To say we need abortions solely for rape and incest is like saying we need prisons for all the people who blow up buildings. I have researched this, thoroughly, and have found that rape and incest account for about 1% of all abortions in the United States. About 6% of all abortions are by people who say they used some form of birth control correctly, and it did not work. That means about 93% of all abortions are by women who either used birth control incorrectly or by women who decided not to use birth control at all. That means the vast majority of abortions are given to women who was either too stupid or too lazy to use birth control. I think you already know how I feel about rewarding stupidity, so this should come as no surprise why this argument angers me.

Another problem I have with abortion is that the terminology conveniently changes. One day it is a fetus, the next day it is an unborn child. If a woman who is two months pregnant goes to get an abortion, it is a fetus. If a man hits a woman who is two months pregnant and causes a miscarriage, it is an unborn child. That man now faces years in prison for murdering an unborn child. Well, what the fuck is it? Either it is an unborn child or a fetus. The definition should not change depending on who does what. I read about a case recently where a woman paid a man to punch her in the stomach so that she could have a miscarriage. The State brought them both up on charges. The judge let the woman go because he said, "She had the right to terminate her pregnancy." The guy, on the other hand, was found guilty of attempted murder of an unborn child. He faces up to 20 years in prison. So, in the logic of the law, a woman can cause harm to her body while she is pregnant because it is just a fetus. If someone else was to cause harm to her body while she is pregnant, it is not a fetus anymore, but an unborn child. This is the most ridiculous shit I have ever heard.

The biggest problem I have with the entire abortion argument is that it removes responsibility and covers for stupidity. Everyone knows, or should know, that if you have sex, there is a possibility a baby could be created. A condom is not that expensive. There are many different forms of birth control that a woman can take to prevent pregnancy. As stated above, a vast majority of abortions are used to end a pregnancy of some dumbass who did not take the time to use proper precautions to prevent a pregnancy from happening.

Do not get me wrong, I do think abortions are necessary. If it is putting the mother's life at risk, then yes, an abortion is a good choice. If the baby will not be healthy or will have some genetic disease or defect, then yes, an abortion is a good choice. When I hear about parents who abused the hell out of their children, then yes, an abortion would have been a good choice. I would rather a child / fetus be destroyed before birth than to have them beaten, starved, assaulted, sexually abused and / or killed. No human should ever have to deal with some of the things some children go through. If a woman is planning on being a horrible parent, then by all means, get an abortion. If a woman is just getting an abortion because she does not want to get fat or because she wants to hang out with her friends, then maybe she should be responsible and take the necessary steps to prevent getting pregnant.

The last thing I will say is this. Personally, I do not care if someone gets an abortion or not. It is not my place to tell anyone what they can or cannot do with their bodies or what is inside it. What I hate is the reasoning and logic that goes into the arguments in support of abortions. Most arguments are feeble-minded and lack consistency.

Guns

There is a huge debate going on right now about guns. Some people feel we should have no guns whatsoever. Some people feel that it is their constitutional right to bear arms. I want to address those that say, "We should get rid of all guns." This is one of the funnier arguments to me, because it is completely unrealistic. The only way to get rid of all guns is to un-invent them. That is right. If you want to do away with all guns, you would have to go back in time and make sure they were never invented. Beyond that, it is impossible to get rid of all guns.

The reason why it is impossible is answered by one simple question, how? How would you get rid of all guns? Would you pass laws to make them illegal? They did that in Chicago and Washington, D.C. a while ago. They made all handguns illegal. Surprisingly, murder rates involving handguns went up. A little secret that the sane world knows that lawmakers seem to not know is that criminals do not give a shit about the laws they pass. You can tell that by the "War on Drugs." Drugs have been illegal, seemingly forever, yet millions of people get their hands on any drug they want on a daily basis. Oh, and in case you were wondering, Chicago and Washington, D.C. changed the handgun law and surprising, the murder rates went down. Sorry, back to the topic at hand. So, making them illegal will not work. Would you create a law that gives a mandatory prison sentence to anyone found with a gun? States already have those and still, gun violence remains. Would you confiscate all the guns in the country? Good luck with that. If you can devise a plan that would guarantee all the guns in the country would be gathered and removed, I would love to hear it.

 I have another question for you. Would you really want to live in a country where only the police and military have weapons? We have all seen the videos of the police beating the shit out of people for no reason. Some of them already feel superior because of their badge. Do we really want to live in a country where these same assholes are the only ones walking around with guns?

 I must confess I am a big believer in guns. No, not because I am Republican or because I live in a trailer park. Hell, I do not even hunt. I believe guns are an equalizer. If a 150 pound woman is being followed by three guys and she feels they intend to do her harm, a gun gives her a chance. Now, I am not saying she should turn around and start shooting them without cause. What I am saying is if they do attack her, she has a reasonable way to defend herself. I have three daughters and I would rather get a phone call from one of them saying, "Hey dad, I shot three guys", then get a phone call from some officer asking me to come down and identify the body. I would rather sit through a trial of one of my daughters trying to explain to a jury why she felt the need to defend herself, than to sit through a trial having to listen to the details of how they raped, tortured and eventually killed my baby.

I want to address the people that feel like guns cause violence. I hate to break it to you, but violence has been around long before guns were invented. The bow and arrow was not invented just to give children something to do at summer camp. Swords were not made razor sharp so they could cut vegetables more efficiently. Humans have been violent throughout history. As long as history has been recorded, there has been war, murder, death. Guns did not turn humans into raging, mindless lunatics. That happened years before them. I believe it was a Tuesday.

The last thing I want to do is respond to those who argue that guns are too dangerous for our society. This society is not mature enough to live with guns. To that I say this society is not mature enough for a lot of things. Yes, we do have a lot of citizens that die from guns. We have more citizens that die from heart disease. Do you want to regulate cheeseburgers as well? There are those that say guns were only invented for one thing, to kill. Are you telling me that two hamburgers with extra cheese, bacon and pickles, large fries deep fried in four day old grease and a large soda that can clean acid off a battery was not? Shit, I am hungry now.

Back to being serious, we cannot take away something from the entire population because a few jackasses are not mature enough to handle it. If that is the case, then we would have to take away a lot of things, starting with alcohol. Everyone likes to quote statistics about guns. Look at the statistics for alcohol. Look at the number of innocent people who die every year from drunk drivers. Thousands and thousands of people every year die because of someone driving drunk. Look at the number of people who commit crimes while under the influence of alcohol. Research it for yourself. I have and the number is quite remarkable. So, let's ban alcohol. No more alcohol in the entire country. You probably just said to yourself, "That's stupid. There's no way banning alcohol will work. People would still continue to drink. They would just acquire the alcohol illegally." That is exactly how I feel about guns.

I am not saying something should not be done about all of the senseless gun crimes. I am not saying we should not make it harder for criminals to get a gun. What I am saying is that we need to take a realistic approach to handling this problem. Just saying, "Get rid of all guns" is just as foolish as saying, "George Bush was a great President!"

Born Gay

This is one of the arguments that I hate the most. There is one side saying that homosexuals are born that way and there is nothing that they can do about it. There is another side saying that it is a choice. They feel people are not born gay. To both sides I say, shut the fuck up.

I am angry at the religious side because they are trying to impose their idiotic beliefs on the rest of the world, yet again. They feel it is a choice because their god would not create anyone to be homosexual. They feel homosexuality is a sin. It is evil and anyone who practices it is evil as well. If you are gay, you will burn in hell forever and ever, and seeing as how their god is just and fair, he would not create you that way and be the cause of your eternal strife. Apparently, he loves you and wants you to be saved. So, logically (and I use that term loosely) homosexuals have to choose to be gay.

     I am angrier at homosexuals for saying they are born gay. Not because they feel that way, but because in responding to the argument at all it gives some credence to the religious bullshit. If you had said nothing, the religious nut jobs would look like the assholes they are. They would be arguing with themselves right now over whether or not they are right. That is not the case though. Right now, they are fighting you tooth and nail over whether or not they are right or you are. You have scientists doing studies and experiments to determine whether or not you chose to be that way. At the end of the day, it does not fucking matter whether or not you chose to be that way or you are born that way.

     This whole entire argument is a waste of fucking time. You want to know why? Even if you are proven right, even if they find the gay gene, it still will not change their mind. They will say you have the gene, but you can pray it away or you can fight the gene and turn straight. Remember, in their world, all things are possible through god. They will open more anti-gay camps to try and convert you to being straight. Pharmaceutical companies will come out with a medication to help you become straight. You will never be accepted in their world, regardless of what proof you have. Do you really think they will accept scientific evidence? Ask atheists how that has been working for them when dealing with religious people.

There was a time in this country when white people thought black people where genetically inferior to them. Science has since proven that to be untrue, yet there are still people, to this very day, that feel white people are genetically better than black people. Despite all the evidence that states otherwise, there are still those that think their race is superior. In short, you cannot fix stupid. Just smile and nod and go on living your life. Entertaining their stupidity just wastes your time and energy.

Seeing that this chapter is called "Counter Arguments", I suppose I have to pick a side and argue it. Here is where I stand on the whole issue. I do not believe a person is born gay. I do not believe attraction is something that is genetic. There are a couple of reasons I feel this way.

The main reason I doubt the "born gay" argument is because I do not understand how it would work. Maybe that is a fault of mine. Maybe it is the fault of the argument itself. How can a gene make you be attracted to someone? Follow me on this. If the gene tells a woman that she is attracted to another women, does it also tell her what type of women she is attracted to? Does the gene specifically implant the idea that she will like fat women or skinny women, short women or tall women? Does the gene tell her she will like girly lesbians or butch lesbians? Does the gene go into that much detail? If not, does that mean the gene tells her she is attracted to all women?

Anyone who knows anything about attraction knows that you are not attracted to someone just because they have a penis or a vagina. All gay men are not attracted to all other men and all gay women are not attracted to all other women.

So, if the gene is not a blanketed "you will like all" of a certain sex, then what is the gene? In order for the gene to make sense, it would have to go into detail as to what a person would like. It would have to specify that a woman would like another woman who is short with long hair. That would be a very interesting gene.

Another reason I question it is because of what some gay people do. Some gay men look, talk, dress and act like a woman to attract another man. Is that not in direct conflict with what the gene would tell a gay man to look for? According to the gene, you are attracted to men because they are men. So, why would a gay man look for another man who looks and acts like a woman? It is the exact same situation when it comes to lesbians. There are a number of lesbians that try their hardest to look and act like a man. Why would a woman genetically predisposed to liking other women be attracted to a woman who is man-like?

The gene also does not account for bisexual people. How can a self-proclaiming born lesbian be attracted to men? How can a gay man that enjoys sleeping with men, also enjoy sleeping with women? Is there a bisexual gene as well?

See, the problem I have with the whole gay gene argument is that it just does not make sense. The people who argue it actually makes it worse. I have heard the stories of women who say they knew of homosexual tendencies from the age of four. When most people cannot remember shit from any age under five, she remembers being gay? When most people are playing dolls or kickball or doctor, she was honed in on her sexuality? Does that not seem just a little bit….wrong?

As of now, there is no scientific proof of a gay gene. Most scientists that have studied it concluded that the environment a person grows up in pays a major role in what they find attractive and what sexual preference they choose. There are many other factors that play a role in sexual preference, but none gene related. If it comes out that they find the gene, I will change my opinion. Until then, I will hold on to the fact that attraction is something you are taught, something that is shaped inside of you from things you see and stories you are told. It is shaped by the events you experience and the life you lead. In my opinion, who someone chooses to be with is a personal choice. The greater point of this chapter is that regardless of that choice, you are in no way wrong for making it.

The Death Penalty

There are a number of arguments that are made for and against the death penalty. Before I get into the arguments, I want to establish that I am for the death penalty in certain cases. If you are a serial killer and have heads and hands in your refrigerator, then there is no rehabilitation for you. If you are raping and/or killing children, then you should have your "life membership" card revoked immediately. I am sorry, but there are certain actions that are so heinous that the only logical punishment is death. There was a guy who was kidnapping, raping, torturing, and then killing women. Do we seriously think prison is a just and fair punishment? What about the parents who abuse their child to the point of death? Would their death not be justice?

I just wanted to let you know my mindset about the death penalty before you read my counter arguments. So, now that we have gotten that out of the way, on to the arguments.

There is an argument that sentencing a person to death is more expensive than keeping them in jail for the rest of their lives. While technically, that is true, it is still the weakest argument there is against the death penalty. Reason being, it is not more expensive simply to house them in prison on death row. The difference in expense emerges from the trial and appeal process. Some states spend three to four times more money to try a death penalty case than a life-in-prison case. If a person is convicted and sentenced to death row, they are automatically given at least two different appeals, if not more. That cost is never calculated in life-in-prison cases because you are not guaranteed an appeal in those cases.

More money is spent on death row trials because they want to get them right. Now, I know some will argue that they do not always get it right. Some will say that the system is too corrupt, too broken to have a permanent, irreversible punishment like the death penalty. Some will argue that in the case the courts arrive at the wrong outcome, a person serving a life sentence still has the opportunity to fight for an overturn of that decision.

My counter argument is simple. Being tried in a capital punishment case gives you the best chance to prove your innocence (if in fact you are innocent). Not only does the state spend a lot more money investigating your case, you are guaranteed at least 2 appeals. That means if the first case does not end favorably, you get two more chances to prove your innocence. You do not get that luxury if you are sentenced to life in prison. They just put you in jail and forget about you. This would explain why some people have been convicted of a crime and it takes ten plus years to get an appeal hearing. I do not even have to bring up the people who have been in jail for 25 to 30 years for crimes they did not commit. They cannot do that if you are on death row. Our system is far from perfect, but death row cases actually are the closest thing we have to perfect in our entire system.

Another argument is that the death penalty does not deter crime. They argue that those States that have the death penalty still have high murder rates. Let's look at a couple of numbers real fast. From 1976 – 2011, there have been 689,475 murders in the United States of America. In the same time period, there have been 1,320 executions in the United States. So, percentage wise, we have executed roughly 0.002% of murderers. That number may be higher, given that I am more than sure there have been murderers that have killed more than one person and we do not catch everyone who commits murder, but I think we can agree on the fact that it is not too much higher. At most, we can say we have executed 0.1% of convicted murderers. With that information I have simple question. Can you stop anything with a method that you utilize less than one percent of the time? If you want the death penalty to deter crime, you have to fucking use it! I am not saying you have to use it for every murder, but you have to use it more than 0.1% of the time if you are trying to use it to deter crime.

There are some people that feel prison is more than enough of a punishment for criminals, regardless of the crime. They feel that taking away someone's freedom is the ultimate punishment. That is a huge joke to me. First, let us look at a very important fact. Over 50% of all prison inmates are repeat offenders. If prison was that fucking bad, the number of people going back would be far less. There have been well documented stories of some of the amenities that prisoners are afforded. Some prisoners live better than hard working citizens. That is a just and fair punishment for someone who decided to take another person's life?

To all those that are against the death penalty, I have a couple of questions for you. What is justice for the family of a murdered love one? The murderer is able to live his life, in remorse or not, while the victim's family tries to piece their lives back together after burying their loved one.

There are some that say killing the criminal will not bring the victim back. That is true. So, do we not punish any criminal because it will not change what happened? Do we not punish a rapist because sending him to jail will not change the fact that the woman got raped? Justice is not about changing what happened. It is about providing a punishment that fits the crime committed. In your world, someone who steals a car, someone who writes a couple of bad checks and someone who kidnaps and murders children all deserve the same punishment. In your mind, that is justice. In my mind, that is insanity.

The biggest problem I have with not having the death penalty is that we live in a world where killers get out of prison. Some of these killers kill again. To me, this is completely unacceptable. Some people's biggest fear is that one day a state will convict and execute the wrong person. My fear is that every time we let a convicted killer out of jail, he or she has the chance to kill again. The difference between my fear and their fear is that there are already a number of cases of convicted murderers killing again, while they are still waiting for the golden case to cement their fears.

The death penalty ensures that a killer will never kill again. He will never have a chance to harm another human being. Yes, the death penalty is final. It is supposed to be. It is just as final as the act they committed. Why should we show mercy to a person who showed none?

In the beginning of this, I said that I believe in the death penalty in certain cases. Let me explain that a little further. If you kill a child, you deserve to die. If you beat a child to death, you deserve to die. If you choke, smother, drown, torment or starve a child to death, you deserve to die. If you attack and kill a senior citizen, you deserve to die. Pretty much, if you prey on and kill the very people this country should protect the most, you deserve to die. We owe it to our children to protect them. We owe it to our senior citizens to protect them. Hell, we owe it to all the innocent people of this country to protect them.

If a dog bites a human, we put it down. We consider it too dangerous, given that it has already attacked a human, and we kill it. We do not give that animal another chance to attack another human. We do that to a dog for a simple bite. Why would it be considered unreasonable to put down a human for ending the life of another human?

Atheists do not value life

There are some religious folks that believe you cannot value life unless you believe in a god. They feel that the only way you can truly understand and respect life is to believe in a creator that gave it to you. This is how they have come to the conclusion that an atheist or non-believer cannot value human life.

This could not be further from the truth. Do you want to know why atheist and non-believers value human life more than anyone else in the world? It is because we do not believe in an afterlife. See, we are not looking forward to a city with streets paved of gold. We do not have a brand new body waiting for us in the afterlife. There are not 40 virgins awaiting our arrival. We are not planning on being reincarnated as another human or a tree. This life is the only life we have and we respect the hell out of it.

In our view, life is a little place I like to call 'reality' - our existence begins at birth and ends at death. Smart atheists make the most of their lives while they are here. They work hard so that they can play harder. They work to make the lives of those around them better because we realize they only have one life. We do not think that a homeless person has treasures stored in heaven. We do not think they are blessed by god and we certainly do not pray for them. We feed them. We try to help them. Not because it is dictated in a book, but because it is the right thing to do. We respect the world we live in because this is the only world we have. We respect our life and the lives of other people because life, here and now, happens only once.

Tax the rich

There is an argument that is being made that the rich people need to pay more in taxes. It is their job and responsibility to pay more in taxes. The poor people are suffering and the rich people just do not want to give up their money. All of our problems would be fixed or at least, begin to get fixed, if we could just get more taxes from those that could spare the money. They do not need all of that money anyway. No one needs that much money. They should just give it to others in the country and if they do not want to do that, the government should just take it by raising their taxes.

I actually love this argument. This argument is fun. Let us start with the obvious. The most reliable number I can find says that the top 1% pays between 25-28% of all federal income taxes. In contrast, in 2009, 51% of all United States citizens paid nothing in federal income taxes and 30% of those people actually got money back in taxes. How can anyone advocate for any group to pay more when 51% of the country is paying nothing? It is funny how the terminology changes from "we" when we are talking about helping the poor or helping the sick or bettering education, to "they" when we start talking about paying for all these things.

People are quick to talk about the tax rate. They look at the tax rate of the rich and the tax rate of the middle class or poor and get completely outraged. We have all heard the stories of how a secretary pays a higher tax rate then her boss. To me, those stories are funny. People are actually trying to compare someone who pays hundreds of thousands of dollars in taxes to someone who would typically get a tax refund or pay nothing. If the boss had a higher tax rate but paid a lower amount of money in taxes than his secretary due to various adjustments, would that be okay? Since some people only seem to be concerned with the tax rate and not the actually amount of money paid in taxes, they should be okay with this, right?

My main counter argument to this whole tax situation is this - money is not our issue. We currently collect more than enough money to accomplish all the things that are needed in this country. The problem is we have jackasses in charge of the money that have no idea what they are doing. You can give a fool a million dollars a year for ten years and in the eleventh year, he will file for bankruptcy because he is broke. You can give a wise man fifty thousand dollars a year for ten years and not only will all his bills be paid up in the eleventh year, he would still have ten thousand dollars saved in the bank. Right now, we have fools in charge and have had fools in charge for many years. They are spending our money on shit we do not want, then turning around and spending money we do not have on shit we do not need.

If you were among the ones investing the majority of tax dollars into a system, would you not pay the most attention to that very system? Let me put it another way. Let's pretend that you live in a country that has a total population of 10,000 people. You are one of the richest people in your country. You gladly pay your taxes to help your country and the people in it. Then you start to notice something: your country is spending your money on ridiculously stupid shit. Would you not get upset? Would you not refuse to pay more money to your government? Any logical person would. In response to your anger, what does your government do? It pushes a campaign to make you the enemy. It is not their fault the country does not have everything the people need, it is your fault.

That is exactly what is happening now. The rich are being crucified for the idiotic decisions the government makes. In 2011, the government spent more on military than the next thirteen countries combined. What logical reason do we have to spend that much money on defense? The only reason I can think of is because the United States is constantly looking to go to war. We may not have money for education, but we sure as hell have money for war. We may not have money for the poor, but we have money to invade other countries. We build and fund military bases all over the world, but we do not have the money to get homeless people off the street.

I touched on this point earlier and I will say it again. The government keeps the population hating each other, so that the focus is not on them. They spent $787 billion in a stimulus package that some argue was a failure. It may have had some benefits, but not nearly the amount of benefits the country should have reaped given the amount of money they spent. We spend money on tank and missiles while school children have to share books. We give financial aid to other countries while our politicians tell us we are broke and need more money.

I am not telling you that you cannot hate the rich. Personally, I do not give a shit about them or their problems. Are some of them assholes? Of course there are. Are some of them liars? Of course there are. Are some of them greedy fucks that try to keep every last penny they have? Both you and I know that there are. My argument is not about the rich being fucking jerks. My argument is that it is delusional to think more money will fix our problems. We clearly have the money. We simply do not have elected officials who make intelligent decisions on what to do with that money.

Socialized Healthcare

There are plenty of arguments for or against socialized healthcare, or as we have come to know it in the United States, Obamacare. I will get into whether or not I agree with it later. What I want to talk about first is the logic, or lack thereof, with some of the arguments.

One of the main arguments for socialized healthcare is the argument surrounding the number of people who are uninsured. Proponents argue that tax payers are paying for the uninsured and healthcare costs are growing. Let me understand this correctly. We, as a society, are tired of paying for medical care for those that are uninsured. They are driving up our healthcare cost because they cannot pay their bills. So, instead of paying for medical services for those 50 million people who are uninsured, we are going to pay for medical services for 300 plus million? Where is the logic in that? We do not want our tax money going to those who do not have insurance, but we will allow our tax money to pay for everyone to have insurance? Can someone explain to me how this makes sense?

Another reason people say we need socialized healthcare is because everyone needs health insurance. The only problem is that this new healthcare plan does not give everyone health insurance. There is an estimated 30 million people who will still be out health insurance. If you look at how the government intends to pay for this new healthcare plan, they are banking on a huge chunk of money coming from companies paying the penalty for not offering health insurance to their workers and from people paying the penalty for choosing to be uninsured. If the goal was to insure everyone, why would you create a plan that does not insure everyone?

Furthermore, if your goal was to insure everyone, why would you create a plan that only works if everyone is not insured?

Yet another argument for socialized healthcare is people feel no one should ever go bankrupt paying for medical bills. While I tend to agree that someone should not lose everything they have just trying to survive, this new Affordable Healthcare Act does not solve that problem. The problem is people, including the people who passed this bill, do not understand how healthcare works. The better your plan, the higher your premium is. Most people cannot afford the high premium, low deductible plan. Most people cannot afford the plan with the low out-of-pocket maximum. I have researched some of the states that already have an insurance exchange and their numbers show that most people get the Bronze plan. It is the plan with the lowest premium (amount you pay per month to have insurance), but it has the highest deductible and highest out-of-pocket maximum.

Here is what can, and probably will, happen. People will have to pay $600-$1000 a month for health insurance on the exchange. Before you say, "Well, the government will subsidize some of that", that is not necessarily true. I believe you only qualify for subsidized healthcare if, and only if, the company you work for does not offer health insurance. If they do, you will receive no government help on your health insurance.

So, let's say a married couple makes a combined $80,000 a year and have one child. They are paying $800 a month for health insurance, which works out to be $9,600 a year for healthcare. They have not even used it yet, and they have already committed almost $10,000 to their healthcare.

Then comes the deductible. This is what the patient has to pay before the insurance pays anything. Typically the deductible kicks in with hospital visits and/or stays, but this can vary depending on the insurance plan. A deductible can be anywhere from $500 to $2,000 or more. Then the plan will typically switch to either a 90/10 split (the insurance company pays 90% of the remaining bill and you pay 10%) or an 80/20 split (insurance company pays 80%, you pay 20%). This will happen until you reach your out-of-pocket maximum, which for a family can easily be $10,000 or more. Now, if one of the parents get sick and accumulates a hospital bill of, say, $200,000, that family would be responsible for as much as $12,000 of that bill. Throw in the $9,600 they are already paying for healthcare and that family will have spent over $21,000 on their healthcare in one year. Is that affordable health care? Are you telling me no family facing that situation would ever dream of filing for bankruptcy, especially taking into account the fact that if someone is really sick they are going to be missing work and receiving either a reduced paycheck or no paycheck at all?

    One more thing, it is possible for prescriptions to have a separate out-of-pocket maximum or not to have an out-of-pocket maximum at all. If the parent from the above example has an on-going illness that requires monthly medication, you can add another $2,000 to $5,000 to their out-of-pocket for the year. As I said, people who make this argument do not seem to understand how insurance works.

    Before I go on I want to clarify one thing. That entire example is based on how insurance is now. From my understanding, the new bill did not really change the format of insurance, just who they could and could not reject, lifetime payouts and who they could and could not cover. If there is anything in the bill changing the format that makes the above argument impossible, then I withdraw the argument.

Let's get to the real reason why our healthcare had to be reformed. It was not because the government gives a fuck about the uninsured or the underinsured. The real reason they had to reform healthcare was because they could not continue to pay for Medicare and Medicaid. It was becoming too much of a financial burden on the country. They had to make a change and make it fast. Thus, the Affordable Healthcare Act was created.

Here is where I get lost. In response to a failing program that the government ran, the government is going to give us..........wait for it......another government program. What? This is like a company making you a car. The car turns out to be a complete piece of shit and in response to your complaints they agree to make you another car. If the government knew what they were doing then the first program would have worked. Please forgive me for not having faith in a government-run healthcare program that is replacing a financially unsustainable government-run healthcare program. There is no reason to believe that the new program will be better than the last one, given the fact the same type of assholes will be running it.

As you can probably tell by now, I do not think this new healthcare plan will work. Even if they made it a completely socialized healthcare system, it would not work in the United States. One of the main reasons is because you cannot control healthcare costs in this country. United States citizens drink too much, smoke too much, work too much, party too much and the average person weighs 1,250 fucking pounds. We are one of the fattest nations in the world. Some of our children are as big as cows. Do you really think our fat ass country cares about their health?

I have heard the argument that all the new preventative programs in the new healthcare bill with improve the health of the nation. This argument assumes that people are complete idiots (not a bad assumption), but I do not buy it. Everyone knows that smoking can cause cancer and other major health problems. A doctor is not giving a smoker ground breaking news when he tells them they should quit smoking. A person who is 450 pounds does not need a doctor to tell them that they need to lose weight. Preventative care is good in theory, but I do not see it changing anything in this country.

Another reason it will not work is because our society fucking sucks. We like to compare ourselves to other countries when we talk about things like healthcare, but healthcare is not the issue. Our society is the issue. In other countries, they make employees exercise every day at work. In this country, the only time you can leave your desk is to go get food and for most of us, you have 30 minutes to get your food, eat, and get back to your desk. People in other countries walk or ride a bike. Here, we drive, call a cab, call a friend, catch a bus or we do not go. In other countries, people actually cook and they like to eat food that is fresh. Here, all of our shit is processed and the only "fruit" most people get ends with 'punch'. In other countries, there are laws that make companies give their employees a certain number of days off. In some countries, it is as much as 30 days a year. Here, our laws demand that companies give us a 15 minute break for every 3 hours worked. In other countries, governments actually create laws that benefit the workers. Here, our government mainly creates laws that benefit the corporations.

We are overworked, overstressed and overmedicated. We eat food with who-knows-what in it and we eat a lot of it. We are lazy. The only time we run is if we are chasing down an ice cream truck or trying to get into a restaurant before they lock the door. We do not get enough sleep. We sit in traffic inhaling exhaust fumes 2-3 hours a day, 5 days a week and we drink shit that could dissolve a nail and we drink it by the liters. If you really think our healthcare system is the biggest problem, then you have no idea what is really going on in this country.

The Conclusion

The reason I wrote this chapter is to show the other side of an argument. I think the problem with this world is that too many people choose a side and then completely ignore any counterpoints. You can take any major issue: abortion, guns, politics, religion, anything. You will always find people have a difference of opinion regarding these things. The problems I have are with the stubborn stances that some people take on issues.

Let me explain. Let's take a problem that divides the country. We can use guns as an example - there are going to be people that land on both sides of the argument. There are going to be people who scream about the constitution and rights. There are going to be people who scream about gun deaths and statistics. The problem comes in when everyone refuses to hear the other side. People are so caught up in fighting for what they perceive to be right, that they lose focus of the ultimate goal -to solve the problem.

The only way to ever truly solve a problem is to look at all the facts. The reason things never get resolved is because people only look at the facts that prove their point. You have one side looking at the fact that people buy guns for hunting, collecting and self-defense. You see videos or read stories daily on how someone stopped a crime by using a gun or defended their family or themselves against a criminal. Guns can and do protect people. That is a fact. Guns can be used safely. That is a fact. You have the other side pointing to the fact that the United States has the highest murder rate of any developed nation. They point to other countries in Europe and Asia and their low murder rate. Those countries have very little gun crimes. That is a statistical fact. They do not have the murder rate of the United States. That is a fact.

Here is where the communication breaks down. Instead of both sides looking at all the facts and saying, "How can we have a country where guns are available to responsible adults, while keeping guns out of the hands of those that should not have them?" Most people immediately jump on the facts that prove their point and completely ignore the facts that counter their point. The whole purpose of having a discussion is to review all of the facts and attempt to come to a reasonable solution. How can you ever accomplish that if you deny that half of the facts even exist?

Fuck You

The church started with a "Fuck you of the day", so obviously I have to include a 'fuck you' section in the bible of the Church. Without further ado, let the fuck you session begin.

Fuck you Penn State. Not only did you have a pedophile roaming your facilities and you did nothing to stop him, it seems like you actually helped him get away with it for so long. Fuck you, for real.

Fuck you Westboro Baptist Church. You are the most useless human beings on the face of this earth. You serve no purpose other than to make people's lives miserable. It seems like you feed on the suffering of people that did nothing to you, or anyone for that matter. Your bigotry is sickening. Your existence is pointless. Please, start committing mass suicide. I assure you, you will not be missed by anyone important.

Fuck you to anyone who has ever said I will never amount to anything. I may not amount to anything, but fuck you for saying it.

Fuck you Boy Scouts of America. You fuckers are / were hiding pedophiles. What in the hell is wrong with you?

As a matter of fact, fuck you to all pedophiles and those who enable them. I hope you all die.

Fuck you racists. Grow the fuck up. There is no room in this world for people believing that your skin color somehow makes you better than other people. Pea-brain, idiotic fuckers - evolve already.

Fuck you to all the people who drive slowly in the left lane. Please people. Left lane fast, right lane slow. Get your bitch ass over to the middle or right lane.

Fuck you Hollywood for making the most horrible movies ever. Even worse, fuck you for remaking classics and fucking them up completely.

Fuck you rapists. "No" means "no" you stupid fuck. And yes, drugging a person counts as rape.

Fuck you to all the people who are sitting at home, on welfare, when you know your ass can work.

Fuck you to all the women who lie about being raped. Not only do you put the man through some bullshit, you make it harder on actual rape victims.

Fuck you to all the men that do not pay their child support. Take care of your children.

Fuck you to all the women who use their children as a weapon against their father. If that man wants to be there for his children, let him. Just because he does not want you anymore, does not mean you should make him suffer by not seeing his children.

Lastly, fuck you to all the people who make life hard or miserable for other people.

What If

I wanted to write something that makes you think outside of the box. Far too many people in this world have their mind set in stone on a lot of issues. I wanted to tackle some of those issues and see if I could make you think a little differently on some things.

Aliens

I know some of you will immediately dismiss the notion that aliens exist. I know some of you will think I am crazy for thinking that aliens may be real. Now, I am not saying that aliens are coming down and abducting people. I am not saying that aliens are coming down and probing people. What I am saying is that given what we know, it is not out of the realm of possibility that there is life on other planets.

What I want to focus on is the universe. There are eight planets in our solar system. At this time, Pluto is not a planet. Who knows, in a couple of years Pluto might be labeled a planet again and we will be back up to nine. As of now, it is eight. And that is just in our solar system – a tiny fraction of the universe! If we just consider the number of planets, is it impossible for there to be life on those other planets? I know some people will say, "Well, life could not exist on another planet." Just because life on other planets may be vastly different from anything we could conceive of, surely does not disqualify the notion that it may be possible or real. Do you really think out of all the other planets and other galaxies that we know of, we are the only living creatures? That is a little conceited, don't you think?

Conspiracy Theories

This is a big one. There are a lot of people that immediately dismiss any idea that a conspiracy theory could be true. Some people get mad. Some people get offended. Some people get flat-out enraged. Now, before I do this one I want to establish, I do not believe all conspiracy theories. Hell, I do not think I believe one conspiracy theory. (For the record, I do not consider the assassination of Kennedy to be a conspiracy theory. If you actually look at the facts of the case, it is not a theory anymore. For those that say I am crazy, look at the evidence. That is all I will say.) With that out of the way, let's begin.

There are a lot of conspiracy theories out there. These are the ones that I know about or care to mention:

9/11 being an inside job.

Landing on the moon was staged.

Assassination of JFK (again, I do not think this is a theory).

Government controls the media.

Private organizations running the world (Illuminati, among others).

Government planning mass murder.

There are many others, but I will stop right there. What I truly get frustrated at when it comes to these theories is how people can immediately dismiss them as being full of shit. It is not that they know for a fact these things happened, they just choose to never think about the possibility that they did not happen the way they were informed. Take, for example, the moon landing. I am not saying the United States government faked it, but how can anyone refuse to believe they *could* fake it? These people are taking on faith that what they were told was true. They have no proof, just the word of someone who said, "This happened." They were not on the moon or on the rocket ship, yet they blindly believe it to be a fact. We have a name for people who blindly believe events off the word of others without any evidence, we call them religious. (And before you say it, a rock and a grainy video is not solid evidence in some people's mind).

The biggest conspiracy theories generally center on the government allowing or organizing a mass murder in order to further their agenda. Some people laugh at the notion that a government would kill their own people. Tell that to those who have suffered at the hands of their government. Stalin killed millions of his citizens either through direct execution, famine, organized massacres or forced labor. The consensus number is around 20 million people. Mao is credited with killing around forty-five million. So, we live in a world where a government killed 20 million of their own people, yet the idea of a government killing 20 of their citizens is ridiculous?

There will be people who say that it was not the United States government. Well, what about Pearl Harbor? The United States received information that an attack from Japan was imminent. They knew at least three hours before the attack that it was going to happen. Yet, the White House chose not to tell anyone. They did not ring any alarms. They did not warn the people in Hawaii that an attack was possible. They did nothing. Some people believe the U.S. government allowed the attack to take place so that they had a reason to join War World II. Over 2,000 people were killed. Over a thousand more people were wounded. Again, it seems a government sacrificed the very citizens they swore to protect. So, in my mind, anything is possible.

One question that gets asked often when discussing conspiracy theories is "why". Why would the government do something like that? To be honest, I do not have a logical reason as to why they would do it. Then again, I do not have a logical reason for the vast majority of murders – why did Mao, Stalin, or Hitler murder millions of people? Asking why to something does not make it untrue. It just means you do not understand the logic behind it.

I want to stress this; I am not saying that any of these theories are factual. I am not saying that any of them are true. What I am saying is that given what we know about governments, instantly disregarding them is foolish.

Reincarnation

Before I start this, I want to say one thing. No one knows what happens when we die. The only sure-fire way to know is to die and stay dead. So, we are all left to speculate about an afterlife or lack thereof. One avenue I would like to explore is reincarnation.

Go with me on this. Let your mind go crazy for a minute. Now, I will not go into all the people who have said they were reincarnated. Obviously, their stories are unreliable. Even though their accounts cannot be fully trusted, reincarnation still is quite interesting. It explains some unexplainable every day phenomena.

Think about all the children that are born with incredible talents. You have three year olds who can play complicated pieces of music. Some may argue that they are just talented. They just know the music. Maybe, just maybe, they learned the music in a past life and still remember it. I know that it is crazy, but it may be the best explanation for a three year old playing Mozart with their eyes closed!

You also have people with multiple personalities. Not only do they switch to a new person, they take on a whole new persona. They have different names, different attitudes, different everything. It could be that they are crazy. It could also be that for whatever reason, they are remembering their past lives and switching on the fly.

Take dreams, for instance. Have you ever had a dream where it was you, but at the same time it was not you? You saw your husband or wife, mother, or daughter, and knew it was them, but they looked nothing like your current husband or wife, mother, or daughter? Have you ever had a dream where you were at a house that felt like home, but you had never been there before? What if your dreams are just visions from your past life? What if you are seeing something you have experienced before? That could explain a déjà vu.

Conclusion

This chapter is not designed to make you paranoid or crazy. Nor did I write this to make you think that I am paranoid or crazy. It was written to open minds just a little bit and make the reader think about things that he or she has not thought about before. Far too many people dismiss things they do not agree with or understand. It puzzles me how some people refuse to think outside of their bubble. If you look at all the things we know about humans, life and the universe, do you really think it is crazy that there may be more going on than we know about?

Revelations

1

I was going to write this long book about what the world has revealed to me. I was going to talk about all of the idiotic things that I have experienced, but I thought of something better. In this chapter, I am going to reveal myself. Many things have transpired in my life that made me who I am. I have seen and heard a lot of things. I have experienced a lot of things that have formed me into the person that I have become. I would like to share those things with you.

If you could not tell by now, I am big on responsibility. Taking care of yourself, your problems, your bills, and your life: these are major issues for me. Owning your mistakes or choices and taking responsibility for your mistakes or choices is also important to me. I guess that started in childhood. If I ever made a mistake in my house, that shit was never forgotten. I was sixteen years old and still hearing about the shit I did when I was ten. Growing up, I learned quickly not to make mistakes.

My friends contributed to my take on responsibility as well. I had the type of friends that laughed at your mistakes. If you fucked up, they made sure you knew it and it would certainly be a source of entertainment. Trying to deny it, pretend it did not happen or make excuses for why it happened only made the situation worse. It was better to simply admit, "Yeah, I fucked up", the joke would be over, the laughter would cease.

I am not saying I had a horrible childhood. It was fun in my mind. The one thing my childhood taught me was responsibility and I truly appreciate that. I had to cook and clean for myself. I had to buy my own clothes and wash them. I was working when I was twelve, but only during the summer. I was working more steadily when I was fifteen years old and have continued ever since. If I wanted something, I had to bust my ass to get it. There was no free ride for me. Working for what you wanted was forced upon me in my teenage years. You may say that is horrible, but I think it was a good thing.

Besides working for what I wanted or needed, my parents showed me how important it was to work, to be productive. They always went to work. There could be four feet of snow outside and my father would be hitching up sled dogs to go to work. My mother had heart surgery recently and was miserable for months. Not because she had had surgery, but because she was missing work. Getting up and going to work has always been an important part of my family's life. Regardless of what is going on, you take your ass to work.

So, now you can see why I get so irritated at people on welfare collecting a check. Hopefully, you understand a little bit more on why I get angry at people for sitting at home, collecting disability because they are too fat or lazy. If you are physically able to get up and go to work, you need to take your ass to work. What angers me more is when I walk into stores and there are people with no legs or no arms greeting me at the door. If they can get up and come to work every day, then everyone should be able to get up and go to work every day. I remember when I was young - there was a guy with cerebral palsy who worked at a gas station. He would go around sweeping the ground and taking out the trash and little things like that. He kept the place clean. He had every reason or excuse not to work, but there he was, every night, keeping the gas station clean and earning his keep. It angers me that more people are not like that guy.

2

I have had very few people in my life that truly loved me. One person that I can say has loved me more than anyone ever has is my mother. No matter what was going on in my life, I knew she loved me. No matter how bad things got in my life, I knew she was there for me. Some of you may say, "Well, that is your mother, she is supposed to do that." You obviously have never met some of the bitches in this world that call themselves "a mother". She truly showed me what love is and I would like to share that with you.

Love is tested by fire. You will know who loves you when all hell breaks loose in your life. There will be many people in your life that claim to love you. You will know who loves you when you need someone to stand by your side. You will know who loves you when you have lost everything. When you hit rock bottom, when you are at your lowest of low, those that help you get up are the ones that love you.

Love is saying "I'm sorry" and meaning it. Love is doing the best you can to make the ones you love happy. Love is sacrifice. Love is accepting the person for who they are. Love is not making a person change for your wants or needs. You would be willing to die for someone you love. You would stand between your love and an angry mob of 100 people and boldly say, "You have to go through me first, and I promise you, you motherfuckers will not make it".

Love makes a person tell you when you fuck up. Love makes a person angry when you do not do your best or when you quit. Love makes a person push you to be your best. Love does not let you sit on your misery. Love does not rejoice when you fail.

The problem that I have with this world is not that people claim to feel love. The problem is that people do not know what love is. People abuse those they supposedly love. People kill those they supposedly love. People will lie to, cheat on, steal from and sell out those they supposedly love. People will do shit purposely that they know the other person hates, yet claim to love them. People will stand by and watch you suffer, yet claim to love you. People will offer you no help in life, yet claim to love you.

Love is more than just a word. Love is more than saying, "I do". Love is something that is felt and shown on a regular basis. Too many people have no idea what love is. They throw the word around, yet they do not truly understand the meaning of the word they say.

3

In my years on this earth, I have learned a lot about friends, which is probably why I do not have many. In my life, my friends have lied to me and on me, stole from me, watched me crash and burn and did nothing to help me out. I have found that many people that call themselves your friend are usually more like an enemy. They do what they can to destroy your hopes and dreams and keep you in the same spot for your entire life. They want to make something of themselves, but they do not want you to make something of yourself.

That is why I am very skeptical when someone talks about their friends. Are they truly friends or are they just leeches, draining your life? The problem is too many people do not know the difference. Just because someone comes over your house and drinks your beer and sits on your couch and watches your television, does not mean they are a friend. Just because someone is always available to go out when you are paying, does not mean they are your friend. Just because you are always there for them when they have a problem, does not mean they are your friend.

I think the biggest thing people need to realize is friendship, just like any relationship, should be a give and take. One day you give, the next day they give. If one side is always giving and the other side is always taking, that is not a friendship. There should also be a huge show of mutual respect. You should respect their feelings, their needs and their property and they should respect yours. There should be agreed upon rules in your friendship. One of the most common would have to be, "Do not try to fuck with my (husband/wife/boyfriend/girlfriend)." I even know some people that would flip out if you tried to mess with their ex. As I said, you have to establish rules.

I am really not trying to overcomplicate a friendship. What I am trying to do is show you what a friendship is not and how to make a good friendship work. I have my doubts about friendship, but that has come from years of experiencing the bad side of it. If you think I am paranoid or too scarred, try talking to people doing ten to twenty years in prison because of their friends.

That is another thing, friends do not put you in fucked up situations. Friends do not put you in situations that may call for you to testify. Friends do not sell you up the river to save their own ass. Friends do not start a fight with fifteen guys at a bar or a club. Friends will not get you shot, stabbed or convicted of anything. Friends should always have your best interest and your well-being in mind. If they do not, then they are not your friend.

4

Another thing I learn throughout my years on this earth is that there will always be division among people. For whatever reason, we, as a society, will always feel the need to divide ourselves from others. I strongly believe you could put ten people in a room for one day and by the end of that day, there will be a minimum of two separate groups. Just look at the amount of shit we divide ourselves with now. We have:

Religious / Non-Religious
Rich / Poor
Black / White
American / Foreigners
Republican / Democrat
Straight / Gay

The two biggest ones are religion and politics. They cause the greatest division among the population and they do it in a way where everyone feels justified in hating and loathing the other side. People want to be separated from "those no-good motherfuckers". They have the idea drilled into their head that their way is right, their way is better, and anyone who does not see it their way is just an ignorant asshole.

I know some of you are thinking, "Yeah, I know. Those (insert whatever group you like) people do that all the time." Well, it is not just those people, it is all of them. For every Republican that says, "Those no good democrats, with their crack addicted welfare babies, are ruining this country", there is a Democrat that says, "Those no good toothless, trailer park republicans, are ruining this country." There are Christians that say, "Those godless, no moral, sinful atheists are ruining this country." Just like there are atheists who say, "Those stupid, judgmental, self-righteous Christians are ruining this country."

Here is what needs to happen. Everyone needs to stop with the stereotypical bullshit. Everyone needs to stop judging and labeling someone that may not agree with their point of view on a particular issue. The most important thing that needs to happen is we need to start looking at people as human, first. If the first thing you just thought was, "Oh, Republicans are not human" or "Atheists are not human", you are part of the fucking problem.

The reason nothing ever gets accomplished anymore is because we do not see humans. We do not see a person. We see a democrat. We see a Muslim. We see a homosexual. What the fuck happened to seeing a person? What happened to looking at a man or a woman and getting to know that man or woman before we pass judgment on them? Is it too much to ask for someone to actually talk to a person before they decide on whether or not they like them? Is it too much to ask for people to act like fucking adults?

I deal with everyone and try to treat everyone equally. I deal with rich and poor, black and white, Asian and Hispanic, straight and gay, Christian and atheist, as I said, everyone. I can do that because I look at the human first. I do not give a shit what you or the rest of the world chooses to label you as, I deal with the person.

If you truly want to change the world, you need to start dealing with the people in it. Majority of the people all over the world have the same concerns. They want to be happy and safe. They want to make enough money to pay their bills and put enough food on the table to feed their children. How about we start changing the world from there?

5

Another thing I learned throughout my life is that people like to bitch and complain and not do anything about what they are bitching and complaining about. You see it all the time. A person will complain about their job, their marriage, their life and make no attempt to make their situation better. I generally hate people like this. There are times though, when they are quite amusing.

The whole 99% and their fight against the "man" - this is one of the more entertaining complaints that I see. You hear them all the time. They are bitching about the rich and how they do not want to help the nation. They complain how poor they are and how the rich are just hoarding all of the money. They scream about how they are living paycheck to paycheck and how the government needs to take their money and give it to the rest of the country. All they do is weep about how unfair things are.

Then, come the day after Thanksgiving, these poor, oppressed, slaves line up like sheep at every store in the country to buy shit they do not need with money they supposedly do not have. They sleep on a sidewalk to be the first in line. They rush through the door, knocking people over and fighting each other all for the chance to give that evil rich man their money. People have literally died in this made rush for pointless shit and the masses have stepped right over them.

This type of insanity usually only happens on the day after Thanksgiving, but the spending insanity continues to Christmas. People max out credit cards and put themselves into debt in order to buy shit for people. They do this all in the name of love. Or is it holiday spirit? Or is it for in worship of god? Well, whatever the reason, it is stupid. After Christmas comes and goes and the bills start coming in, these geniuses start bitching and complaining again. Suddenly, they remember that they hate the rich and they are reminded of their oppression when the credit card companies demand payment.

When I look at the situation, it is simple to me. If you hate the rich so much, then stop buying their shit. Stop making the rich richer with your money. That may mean you have to go without the latest gadget or you may not be up to date in the fashion department, but so what? You hate the rich, remember? You feel they are destroying your life, right? If so, you should have no problem stopping your support of them. Then again, that would require you to actually do something other than complain. That would require you to make sacrifices in your life for a cause that you believe in. Many never do that though. Many just stick to crying about it. It is easier and it does not require you to do anything.

The 99% are not the only ones. Those who cry about global warming while not changing their consumption habits are funny as well. They leave every light on in their house and have their heat on 85 degrees in the winter, yet cry that we are melting the North Pole. You have those people that buy cars that get ten miles per gallon, and then bitch about gas prices. You have fat people that cry about losing weight, yet eat four double cheese burgers for dinner every night. This list could go on seemingly forever, but you get the point.

As simple as I can say this, if you do not like something, do what you need to do to change it. If you are not going to change it, then shut the fuck up and stop complaining about it.

6

The last thing I want to reveal about myself is that I want to be someone important. I really, really want to "make it". I grew up with this feeling that I am a nobody, that my life did not matter. I have always had the feeling that I would never accomplish anything. I would be just another person who came, lived, and died. In twenty or thirty years after my death, no one will even remember my name.

I turned to religion to feel important. Obviously, that did not stick. The problem I had with religion is that I really believed it. I mean, I was all in on religion like it was a four-of-a-kind. The problem with that is if you really believe in a god, you expect god to do things like the bible says he would. I prayed over empty containers, expecting for food to appear. I prayed over my children, expecting them to get better when they were sick. I prayed my ass off. I believed the bible when it said if you have the faith the size of a mustard seed, you can tell this mountain to move into the ocean and it will.

Then one day I woke up and realized it was all bullshit. Most pastors or preachers are just money hungry leeches that will tell you anything they can to maximize what goes into the collection plate. I also come to realize that my life was up to me. I had to do everything for myself with no help from a god. If I wanted food, I had to take my ass to the store and get food. If I did not want to get sick, I had to take care of myself or go to the doctor. If I wanted to accomplish something, I had to do it. So, logically, if I am doing everything for myself, what do I need a god for?

That ended my religious belief, but I still wanted to be someone in this world. So, I thought the best way to make it is to be myself. Thus, I started to put a lot of time and energy in the Church. Truth be told, this all started as a little joke. It has grown and grown and now I have a number of people who love to hear what I say and how I feel. We may not agree on everything, but it is still fun to have the conversations.

Sorry, back on topic. So, I want to make it. Mainly because I feel it would give me the best opportunity to promote change in society. Generally speaking, no one really listens to someone who is not considered important. If I want to make the changes necessary for this world to be a better place for everyone, I have to get myself in a position where I am heard by everyone. That is my goal. I want to make it to the mountain top so that I can help pave the way for anyone else who wants to make it to the mountain top. I will make it one day and I will do my best to make sure everyone can get there as well. That will be one crowded fucking mountain top!

www.ingramcontent.com/pod-product-compliance
Lightning Source LLC
Chambersburg PA
CBHW051836090426

42736CB00011B/1831